IF IT'S TRIVIA ABOUT BALTIMORE IT'S FAR FROM TRIVIAL

BY DENNIS McCLELLAN

Published and Printed in the United States of America
in 1984 by:

      Schneidereith & Sons, Inc.
      2905 Whittington Avenue
      Baltimore, Maryland 21230

Library of Congress Cataloging in Publication Data

    McClellan, Dennis N.
      If It's Trivia About Baltimore, It's far
      from Trivial

      1. Baltimore — Questions and answers
    I. Title

Library of Congress Catalog Card Number 84-51909

ISBN: 0-9602304-2-4

Dedicated to
the Trivial People and Events that have
made my life everything it has been
— and to
Eric, Mark and Cindy
who have made it even better!

Preface

Do you know that former Baltimore Colt, Alan Ameche was nicknamed "The Horse?"

Are you aware that Francis Scott Key wrote what was to become "The Star-Spangled Banner" while being detained aboard a British ship?

Maybe you know that Babe Ruth, a local boy, was among the first five men elected to the Baseball Hall of Fame in 1936.

Well, the fact is that you might know a great deal about Baltimore. You might be able to rattle off statistics about the ORIOLES, the COLTS, the PREAKNESS, the BLAST, the SKIPJACKS, the BULLETS, the CLIPPERS, and other sports teams. It is possible that you can quote the works of H. L. MENCKEN, OGDEN NASH or HYMAN PRESSMAN. Maybe you know that at one time Baltimore was the STRAW HAT capital of the nation *OR* that the *CONSTELLATION* was built with 38 guns *OR* that the city had two men who did more for children — ENOCH PRATT and JOHNS HOPKINS — than any two other and that both were childless.

If you knew these facts or if you know more about Baltimore — that's great.

All this stuff that you know is called TRIVIA . . . often defined as "unimportant facts, matters or information that have little or no real significance." Things that are trivial are supposedly without novelty or freshness — things that are commonplace.

If this is true, it is then difficult to explain the popularity of trivia books and games. America has been smitten with trivia. It comes in all forms: facts, questions, statistics, etc. Not everyone cares,but it is a fact that more males are conceived and born than females. And not everyone can answer: Who portrayed Morticia Addams on the TV series "The Addams Family?" Why, the late Carolyn Jones of course. Then there are those who know that historical statistics indicate that there were three United States presidents who had last names that had only four letters. Did you recall Polk, Taft and Ford?

Well, *IF IT'S TRIVIA ABOUT BALTIMORE IT'S FAR FROM TRIVIAL* is different from any other trivia book. This book deals exclusively with BALTIMORE.

Be bold! Take a chance! Check yourself out. You might be very surprised how much you really do know *and* do not know about Baltimore. You may not know everything found here; but that's okay. A great deal of work went into making this not only challenging but informative.

IF YOU WANT TO:

HOW TO SCORE YOURSELF

If you decide to test yourself and play against others, you might use the following scoring procedure:

There are a total of 560 questions in this book (not including the factual briefs found at the bottom of most pages). For each answer you get correct, give yourself two points; zero is credited to incorrect answers. Compute the total score for correct answers and then divide the total by five.

The resulting score can be checked against this less-than-scientific check list:

		SCORE	
EXCELLENT	196–224	TRUE BALTIMOREAN
GREAT	147–195	*6th* GENERATION
GOOD	98–146	SHORT TIMER
FAIR	49– 97	JUST A TOURIST
POOR	0– 48	ROBERT IRSAY'S GET OUT OF TOWN AWARD

Don't Take It Too Seriously. Just Have Fun!

CONTENTS

No, He Wasn't Hiding in Baltimore 1

He Never Lost His Sense of Humor 2

Can You Ever Really Be too Fast? 3

Well, So Much for Rehabilitation.. 4

The Leg Bone's Connected to the.. 5

They're Dying to Get in 6

Sit Down and Take a Load off Your Feet 7

A Horse, a Horse, My Kingdom 8

Maybe You Can Go Home Again.. 9

So, What Else Did They Talk About?... 10

So Much for Meditation 11

Disasters, Disasters, Baltimore Has Survived Many, but............................. 12

Father Knows Best 13

Every Kid Deserves to Learn to Read. That is the
       Responsibility of any Good School.. 14

It could Have Been Worse 15

He Was on the Ball 16

Boy, Aren't You Glad He Didn't Live in Baltimore? 17

But Everyone Does It 18

A Hypochondriac's Premature Death 19

When Are You Old Enough?.. 20

It's Not How You Play the Game... 21

At Least It Wasn't a Shotgun Marriage.. 22

History in the "Making"... 23

Just Wait Long Enough and the Weather Will Change 24

Without a Trace 25

The Sports of Kings 26
But Could He Act 27
Just as Good as a Set of Fingerprints 28
Oops! 29
Sight for Sore Eyes 30
And You Thought She Could Only Sing 31
The Defense and the Prosecution were Both Wrong 32
Nobody's Perfect 33
He Was Not Easily Impressed 34
Too Much Can Cause Cavities 35
Fact or Fiction 36
Give Me Strength 37
Who Made a Monkey Out of 38
Well ! ! ! ! ! 39
And the Legend Goes On and On 40
I Didn't Hear Anything, Did You? 41
But I Didn't Know What I Was Doing 42
The Final Curtain 43
The Butler Did It 44
Maybe He Should Have Answered His Fan Mail 45
The Other Side of the Street 46
You Know Where to Find Me 47
I Didn't Know That 48
Sloppy, Sloppy 49
Things That Go Bump in the Night 50
Can We See into the Future? 51
It May Be Chile, but It Sure Is Hot 52
A Lot of Money for Those Days 53
Even Fillmore Would Have Liked the Honor 54
Two Baltimore Failures in One Lifetime Is Enough 55
Baltimore Has Always Had Someone with a Comment on Any Subject .. 56
Talk About Strong School Ties 57
Statistics About the Renaissance City 58
It's Hard to Keep Them Around When They Don't Want to Stay 59
The *Sun* Newsboy Band Excursion 60

Right Name — Wrong Reason 61
Eyewitness to History in the Making.. 62
C.O.D. Presidency... 63
Not Quite on the Top 40.. 64
The Great Fire of 1904 was Terrible, but 65
It Doesn't Matter How You Spell It 66
A Sad End for One of Baltimore's Outstanding Visitor—Personalities.................. 67
The Man Was Multi-Talented... 68
A Dead Woman's Legacy 69
Oh, Those Roaring Twenties... 70
Another First for Baltimore 71
We Ought to Be in Pictures... 72
$50 or $100, It Was an Important Beginning... 73
The Son of a Baptist Minister and the Actor's Son.................................. 74
Yes, This Is Trivial 75
You Won't Have Old What's His Name to Kick Around Any More......................... 76
Ex Parte Merryman.. 77
Tidbits 78
What Authors Do Other Authors Read? 79
There's Nothing New Under the Sun 80
Baltimore Girls to the Rescue... 81
Firsts, Firsts, More Baltimore Firsts 82
Lesser Known Facts About the Preakness 83
The Unsolved Murder 84
The Unsolved Murder (Continued) 85
Some Feel That the Local Man Never Died That Day................................... 86
This Girl Really Got Around.. 87
The Strange Events of Mrs. Carter's Voyage 88
Pure Sports! 89
Pure History! 90
The Finer Arts! 91
Pure Baseball!... 92
Baltimore Dates and Events 93
Pure Football! 94
Pure Preakness! 95

Expert Level Baltimore Trivia   96
Super Expert Level Baltimore Trivia   97
Expert Level Baltimore History Trivia   98
Very Serious Football Trivia   99
Expert Level Mixed-Bag Baltimore Trivia 100
Answers to Questions 101
Index 135

Questions

1. Name the last Baltimore Oriole pitcher to hit a grand-slam home run in a World Series.

2. Nearly 4,000 Baltimoreans gathered to celebrate the ratification of the United States Constitution by Maryland in 1788. Where did they have their party?

3. In the motion picture "Animal House," Delta T X fraternity at Faber College was led by President Robert Hoover. What happened to him in the years after he left those ivy-covered halls?

4. What is Baltimore's longest street?

5. In 1927 the composer of "How Ya Gonna Keep 'Em Down On The Farm?" and "My Buddy" wrote a song that broke one of the cardinal rules of song writing. However, Gene Austin of Baltimore recorded it — helping to sell many of the 12 million copies. Name the song.

No, He Wasn't Hiding in Baltimore . . .

In 1946 Jerry Voorhis, a wealthy liberal, decided to seek a sixth term as representative from the 12th Congressional District of California. The Republicans had no one to oppose him and organized the "Committee of One Hundred" to locate a candidate. Twenty-six newspaper ads were placed that read:

> "Wanted: Congressman candidate with no previous political experience to defeat a man who has represented the district in the House for 10 years. Any young man, resident of district, preferably a veteran, fair education, may apply for the job."

Eight men applied and were rejected. At the suggestion of the former president of Whittier College, a lawyer and former navy vet was sought out and finally found in Baltimore. The 33-year-old had voted for Dewey in 1944. He was returned to California and selected to run against Voorhis. Although he liked Voorhis personally — especially due to his anti-Communist positions — the young man set out to destroy him and did just that. Voorhis was attacked as a "red tool" and when the votes came in, he had lost 49,431 to 64,784. This was just the beginning of what was to be an unbelievable political career for the man found in Baltimore: Richard M. Nixon.

2

Questions

1. Originating in Baltimore, it became the oldest non-news TV show in the nation. Name it.

2. On December 26, 1965 the Colts lost to the Green Bay Packers in sudden death (13-10) on a disputed field goal. With two quarterbacks already injured, what player filled in with plays written on a wristband? Who were the injured quarterbacks?

3. What is the statue of George Washington holding in his right hand atop the Washington Monument?

4. After arriving in Baltimore, Edgar Allan Poe entered a short story contest sponsored by *The Saturday Visitor* and won a first prize. Name the story that was submitted and won the young author a prize worth $50 — a story that told of a ghost ship and its sinister crew.

5. Her real name was Fanny Belle Fleming and she began her professional career at the age of 16. She was the reported, one-time mistress of Louisiana Governor Earl Long. She was perhaps the biggest draw "the Block" ever had. Name her.

He Never Lost His Sense of Humor . . .

In 1948 Baltimore was shocked to learn that H. L. Mencken had suffered a crippling stroke. Undaunted, he worked hard at his therapy; however, he was not able to read or write. Each day his brother August brought him his usual Havana cigars and stein of drink. But life was never the same.

Once a guest stopped by for a visit. During conversation, Mencken was asked about a friend and writer, Edgar Lee Masters. "I believe he died," the guest asked, "in 1948, didn't he?" Mencken looked up, his eyes twinkled and he replied, "Yeah, I believe he died the same year I did."

Questions

1. In 1898 Gertrude Stein arrived in Baltimore to study. Study what and where?

2. Name the 1979 winner of the Preakness, the owners of the horse, and the jockey who rode into the winner's circle.

3. According to political analyst, William Safire, to whom should we attribute the following words and phrases: "radic-libs, effete snobs, instant analysis, household word, and nattering nabobs of regalism?"

4. What member of the Baltimore Bullets held the record for the most points scored in an overtime period in pro basketball? (Hint: the record is shared.)

5. Radio station WEBB was owned by what recording star who sold it for a reported $435,000 — money that was needed to repay back taxes to the federal government on several business interests?

Can You Ever Really Be too Fast . . .

Perhaps the greatest pitching legend to ever pick up and throw a baseball and never succeed in the major leagues was a farmhand for the Baltimore Orioles. His name was Steve Dalkowski and he was awesome.

His strikeout ratio was something else: 1,396 in 995 innings in the minors (1950's and 1960's).

He was also known for his walks: 1,345.

Of the 10 fastest men ever timed, Dalkowski was checked at 93.5 miles per hour. The hardest fact to face for Steve was, that out of those 10 fastest men, he was the only one of them to not succeed in the majors. He had a minor league record that was a mere 46-80. However, he did make the *Guinness Book of World Records* for his distinction.

4

Questions

1. If you had attended the funeral service for Charles Carroll of Carrollton in 1832, in what religious structure in Baltimore would you have been sitting?

2. F. Scott Fitzgerald completed a number of short stories in 1935, while living at what Charles Street residence?

3. Name the Baltimore based company whose 1977 annual report (all 22,000 copies) were processed to give off the aroma of cinnamon.

4. Robert Garrett was a Baltimore banker and Olympic winner. In 1896 he won an event — an event that he had never seen prior to the games, let alone practiced it. What was Garrett's event?

5. On March 30, 1983 the *Pride of Baltimore* became the first ship of its type to ever do something. What did she do at noon in California?

Well, So Much for Rehabilitation . . .

Joseph Thompson Hare was probably the single most celebrated of America's highwaymen of the early 19th century. He led a gang of cutthroats along the Wilderness Road and the Natchez Trace for years, plying his number one skill — robbery.

Hare was an elegant dresser, a dandy who had grown up in the slums of Baltimore. His earliest lawless adventures took place in New Orleans and gravitated back toward Maryland.

He lucked out in 1813 when, after being captured and sentenced to the gallows, he was given a five-year prison term instead. After serving his time, Joe returned to a life of crime. Prison had taught him nothing about crime, except that it might pay.

He made $16,000 by robbing the Baltimore night coach near Havre de Grace, but left a good trail. Two days later he was captured. It seems that being a dandy had its drawbacks. Poor old Joe, to keep in style with fashion trends of the day, he went shopping for an officer's coat. He found one for a mere $75, but while trying it on, he was spotted. Unfortunately, it cost him more than the price of a coat. He was hanged on September 10, 1818, after leaving a note in his cell. In part it read: " . . . as it is a desperate life, full of danger, and sooner or later it ends on the gallows."

Questions

1. Reggie Jackson, a one-time Oriole, has been on two different teams that brought home the World Series: the Oakland A's in 1973 and 1974 and the Yankees in 1977 and 1978. What other player, an Oriole, could make that claim?

2. The first arrived in the port of Baltimore from India in 1772. In 1828 the first factory to produce them was built and began production — making Baltimore the capital of what product?

3. When the Mondawmin Mall was dedicated in 1956, a poem was read as part of the ceremonies. From what famous poem does the word "Mondawmin" come?

4. Name the famous American motion picture actor who was born on Argyle Avenue in Baltimore.

5. What was MK-ULTRA?

The Leg Bone's Connected to the . . .

When Robert Burger walked into Littlepage's Furniture Warehouse on February 9, 1984 to do a routine cleaning of the boiler system, he had no idea of the events that lay ahead of him. As Gomer Pyle might have said: "Surprise, surprise, surprise!"

As he was scraping debris from the system, he found the completely decomposed body of a man that had probably been there for months. Over the years pigeons had the gall to get caught in the elevator shaft and die. But this was the first time that a human had made such an appearance at the building at 1300 West Baltimore Street. The body discovered by Burger was mere bones with small scraps of cloth clinging to them. It was suspected that the skeletal remains represented what was left of a male in his mid-20's who died after becoming wedged in the exhaust tower of the 70-foot chimney. Unfortunately for the would-be burglar, the tower which measured 14 inches, narrowed to only 12 inches as it approached the boiler. This spelled the end for the young man whose body would be left undiscovered for months — only to be found accidentally by Robert Burger.

6

Questions

1. What is "Baltimore clay?"

2. Where would you find the grave of H. L. Mencken?

3. The Milton Inn, a popular eating place in the Baltimore area, was once the Milton Academy — a school for boys that dates to about 1740. Name its most notorious student.

4. Ernie Barnes was drafted by the Colts in 1960. What was his relationship to TV producer Norman Lear?

5. "Oh Baltimore — Man it's hard to live." These words appeared on a recording by what singer-composer?

They're Dying to Get in . . .

Near Baltimore sits one of the most unique places in the entire United States. Bonheur Memorial Park could be called a cemetery with a real difference.

This pet cemetery has advertised itself as America's largest and finest memorial park for pets. In 1978 a startling reality took place: it became the first pet memorial park in the nation to seek and receive approval to bury pets and their owners side by side. Local Howard County "People" cemeteries objected. However, the transition took place.

On special occasions, such as birthdays and death dates, candles are lit. Some owners have taken their pets home after the animals are placed in caskets, prior to burial. Owners see themselves as trendsetters and have initiated a grave marker project. The plan is to raise enough money to place a special marker at the grave of Mary Ann, a three-and-one-half-ton elephant buried at Bonheur in 1948.

It is calculated that the cemetery has enough space for some 900 humans and 1600 animals.

Questions

1. The Beatles made two appearances in Baltimore during their initial exposure to American audiences. Where and when did they appear?

2. Name the oldest building in the United States used continuously for medical education.

3. Daniel and Philip Berrigan, joined by other Vietnam protesters, destroyed local draft files in 1968. What did the group become known as?

4. In 1976 Baltimore actress Bess Armstrong got her debut on what television series that ran for only one year?

5. The United States flag is authorized to fly both day and night over the Capitol in Washington, D.C., the World War Memorial, the grave of Francis Scott Key, and what fourth location?

Sit Down and Take a Load off Your Feet...

The year was 1929 and "Shipwreck" Kelly became a new American hero and celebrity when he set a record for sitting atop a flagpole for 145 days. In Baltimore, 15-year-old Avon Foreman made his own fame.

The boy set up an 18-foot hickory pole in his back yard and perched on top. He gained the attention of Mayor William F. Broening who wrote him a letter. It said in part:

> "The grit and stamina evidenced by your endurance from July 20th to 30th, a period of 10 days, 10 hours, 10 minutes, and 10 seconds atop of the 22-foot pole in the rear of your home shows that the old pioneer spirit of early America is being kept alive by the youth of today."

Other kids followed Avon's lead, and during one week in 1929, Baltimore had no less than 20 pole-sitting youth (17 boys and 3 girls).

8

Questions

1. What was Gentleman Jim Corbett's connection with the Baltimore Orioles?

2. In 1952 an ice show was held at the Fifth Regiment Armory on Howard Street. It was a sellout and temporary stands were erected to handle the overflow. Just prior to the start of the show, some of these stands collapsed injuring more than 250 people. Due to lawsuits, the entire review was eventually canceled and its national run was brought to a halt. Who was the Olympic skating champion who headed the show?

3. The Baltimore City Council passed a resolution in 1972 banning the use of two terms by police when describing the lawless elements of the city. What were the two terms?

4. In the movie "Diner," what was the name of the diner where the kids hung out?

5. Captain John Smith is given historical credit for discovering the Patapsco River. What was the name for the river?

A Horse, a Horse, My Kingdom . . .

American artillery officers of the early 19th century were impressed with the Napoleonic system of artillery and urged its introduction in this country. The system made use of horse-drawn guns that raced with foot soldiers from one front to another as needed.

On April 12, 1808 an Act of Congress allowed for the inclusion of a regiment of light artillery in the army. Captain George Peters was given command of the battery. It was issued sufficient horses to mount itself in the true Napoleonic style and on July 4, 1808 was prepared to test its worth. On that day, the battery staged an impressive demonstration for Congress.

A march was conducted from Baltimore to Washington at a speed of six miles per hour. Good impressions aside, when President Jefferson left office, the project was declared a waste of money and scrapped. The horses were sold off.

Unfortunately, a few years later the country found itself at war with England. And although the battle for Baltimore was an American victory in 1814, the horse artillery could have made a brief war even more brief.

Questions

1. Under what conditions was Eddie Murray ejected for the first time from a major league game?

2. Baltimore had two famous "Tom Thumbs" in its history. What was so unique about each of them?

3. He was an ambulance driver in World War I, along with such other future greats as Walt Disney, E. E. Cummings, Ernest Hemingway, W. Somerset Maugham, and Archibald MacLeish. He authored more than 30 books and died at his Cross Keys residence in 1970. Who was he?

4. Name the personality who was raised in Baltimore, died in 1937 in Clarksdale, Mississippi, and is buried in Sharon Hill, Pennsylvania.

5. What Baltimore Colt holds the team record for the most touchdowns scored by a running back in an NFL season?

Maybe You Can Go Home Again . . .

Thomas Wolfe, born in 1900 in Asheville, North Carolina, was one of the most influential writers of this century. With writings full of Southern emotionalism, Wolfe may have been the chief spokesman for the artistic beliefs of the 1930's. While on a trip to the northwestern United States and Vancouver, he was taken quite ill.

After an eight-week stay in a Seattle hospital, it was still a mystery as to the cause for the shadow that appeared on X-rays of his right lung. His sister was advised to take him to Johns Hopkins Hospital across the continent. There he was treated by Dr. Walter Dandy who relieved Wolfe's intracranial pressure by trephination.

On September 12, 1938 the doctor performed a craniotomy and declared the case hopeless. Wolfe, he discovered, had miliary tuberculosis of the brain. An old lesion of the lungs had been disturbed by the recent illness (pneumonia), and the microorganisms had been released into the bloodstream. Wolfe was given all possible care, but he could not be saved. He died on September 15, 1938.

Wolfe's body was sent back to North Carolina from Baltimore and buried in Riverside Cemetery in Asheville. The return of the body to Wolfe's hometown proved that Wolfe was wrong when he titled his epic novel, *You Can't Go Home Again*.

10

Questions

1. The United States went to war in 1846 — the same year Liszt wrote his First Hungarian Rhapsody. It was also the same year that the first message was ever transmitted over wires by a United States president. That message was sent to what Baltimore location by what president?

2. Name the horses ridden to victory in the Preakness by Eddie Arcaro.

3. What was the original name of Baltimore Polytechnic Institute when it first opened in 1884?

4. Where would you find Fuselage Avenue, Propeller Drive and Cockpit Street?

5. Name the sporting event that (1) had a purse of $60,000, (2) was shown live in Europe via CBS-TV's "Sports Spectacular," and (3) attracted Great Britain's Prince Philip.

So, What Else Did They Talk About?...

Ron Wood, guitarist for the "Rolling Stones," sat in the green room awaiting his turn to be interviewed on the ABC's "Good Morning America" show. As he waited, Wood got into a brief conversation with the other personality awaiting his interview with David Hartman.

After a short time, Wood asked the man if he had any vodka with him. "No," replied the other man. With that, the young rock musician walked out of the room and retrieved a bottle from his car.

The other man finally went before the cameras and discussed his chances of being elected to the Baseball Hall of Fame. At the time, he had no way of knowing that he would be elected on the first ballot. He also did not know that when he returned home to Baltimore his daughter would be disappointed that her father had failed to obtain an autograph from the rock star.

Greatness, like beauty, is in the eye of the beholder. It makes you wonder if any of Ron Wood's friends were disappointed that he had failed to get Brooks Robinson's autograph that fateful day in 1983.

Questions

1. Coors advertises that its beer is "Brewed With Pure Rocky Mountain Spring Water." Schlitz is "The Beer That Made Milwaukee Famous." Budweiser is the "King of Beers." And Black Label says that it is "The World's Leading Internationally Brewed Beer." What was Mr. Boh's claim?

2. In the motion picture "Rosemary's Baby," Mia Farrow played the role of Rosemary Woodhouse who had come to New York from Omaha. She met and married Guy who had made a pact with the devil. Who was the actor who portrayed this character in the movie — who we are told came to New York from Baltimore?

3. What national problem held up the formal dedication of The Peabody Institute?

4. What are Congreve rockets?

5. What locally-made product made its TV debut as the sponsor of the 1950's program, "Person to Person," that starred Edward R. Murrow?

So Much for Mediation . . .

On July 6, 1877, strikers on the Baltimore and Ohio Railroad spontaneously walked off their jobs, although no strike order had been called. Unrest had been brewing for some time over wage cuts. Railway workers on the East Coast were quite hostile, and when the mess hit Baltimore, all hell broke loose.

Governor John Carroll called out the National Guard to protect the railroad's property at Cumberland. When the soldiers arrived in Baltimore, they were met with mob-filled streets and angry protesters throwing cobblestones. The soldiers finally opened fire on the crowds and 10 civilians were killed. Federal troops were hustled into the city in a few days, and soon there were some 500 armed troops on duty. During the Baltimore rioting, 50 people died in 4 days.

12

Questions

1. Name the 24-year-old New Englander who spent 49 days in a Baltimore jail for libeling a local merchant involved in the selling and shipping of slaves and who vowed to spend the rest of his life in efforts to put an end to slavery.

2. What local singer, actor, playwright, and freelancer released the yuletide recording, "Crabs for Christmas?"

3. In 1880 a world famous structure was brought to Baltimore and set up at Lombard, Howard and Liberty Streets for the city's Sesquicentennial. Today it can be seen in New York's Central Park. Name it.

4. The Baltimore Colts appeared in what 1977 movie supposedly in a playoff against the Los Angeles Rams in what was called "Championship 10?"

5. Dr. Russell S. Fisher, Maryland's former chief medical examiner, appeared prominently in the foreword of which of Erle Stanley Gardner's mystery novels?

Disasters, Disasters, Baltimore Has Survived Many, but . . .

In numbers of lives lost, the worst disaster took place before the Civil War on April 14, 1842 on the water. Early that morning a 180-foot wooden, side-wheel steamer, the *Medora*, lay alongside John Watchman's wharf. This was going to be her maiden voyage. All she needed was her crew and passengers.

The *Medora* was owned by the Baltimore and Norfolk Steam Packet Company. Her officials gathered at the wharf with their families and friends for the big occasion. Within moments, the festive air was turned into a mob scene; shocked and screaming people could not believe their eyes and ears.

Just as the steamer was pulling away from the dock, just as the paddle was making a revolution, the boiler exploded and ripped through the bow. The boiler hurtled into the air and fell back onto the deck, sending scalding steam over all who were near. The craft went to the bottom of the Patapsco with many of its 79 passengers and crew. Twenty-six were killed and thirty-eight were injured.

City officials followed a common practice of the day and fired cannon throughout the day — hoping that the explosions would dislodge any body trapped on the river bottom. One of the most unusual events of the day followed the initial explosion. The wife of one of the crew members rushed to the water's edge, just after the explosion and spotted a human hand floating amongst the debris. On the hand was a ring — with her husband's name on it. In time, the *Medora* was raised from the river, rebuilt and renamed the *Herald*. The steamer operated until 1885.

Questions

1. What United States president went to college in Baltimore? What was the highest degree awarded him?

2. Over the years many baseball teams have won 100 games or more and have not won the pennant. It has happened to the Orioles just once in modern times. When? To whom did they forfeit the title?

3. Name the prolific artist who signed her first works "George" because she wasn't impressed with women artists and their work and who today has a tremendous following.

4. The oldest investment banking house in the United States is found in Baltimore. Name it.

5. The Bromo Seltzer Tower was built shortly after the Great Fire of 1904. It is a copy of what other structure?

Father Knows Best . . .

The Interpretation of Dreams by Freud was a most popular book during the 1920's. It had a great impact and influence on contemporary ideas. At the same time, Dr. John B. Watson of Johns Hopkins University created his own form of sensation.

He created "behaviorism." Actually, he borrowed — and borrowed freely — from the research of others to create his theory. To what he borrowed, Watson transferred techniques and assumptions from animal psychology to human psychology — as if no important differences existed between the two. He openly denounced other psychologists who were trying to unravel instinct, the mind, emotions, and the like. He became rather famous. Eventually Hopkins fired him.

In 1925 he published *Behaviorism* and was hailed for publishing "perhaps the most important book ever written." Meanwhile, the United States government published "Infant and Child Care," the most widely read government publication of its day. It made use of Watson's regimen for raising children.

What did Watson have to say on the subject of child rearing? Well, he wrote that children should be fed by the clock, they should never be allowed to cry for attention, that self-indulgence of any kind must be disallowed, that one should never argue with a child, and he stressed that sentimentality should never be allowed to enter the picture.

14

Questions

1. In 1928, numerous graduates of Douglass High School went on to bigger and better things. Two of these went on to really bigger things: one went into law and has been involved in some of the nation's most important court decisions; the other went into music and has had a major impact on Broadway, Hollywood and popular music for over half a century. Name these classmates.

2. Name the Baltimorean who gave Gina Shock of the recording group, the "Go Go's," her start.

3. Who is quoted as saying, just before he died: "I dine tonight in Baltimore — or in Hell!"

4. Name the only Preakness winner with a three-word name — all words the same.

5. Where did the Waverly section of Baltimore get its name?

Every Kid Deserves to Learn to Read. That Is the Responsibility of Any Good School . . .

In 1879 the McGuffey Reader was the single most important educational influence on American children. The series of six basic elementary readers and a spelling book offered children a taste of classic writings — writings that are practically unknown among even the best of well-read adults in today's society.

Baltimore writers made contributions to the pages of the readers. Some of the writers had been long dead. John P. Kennedy (1795–1870), politician and writer, was born in Baltimore and graduated from the College of Baltimore. He served on many levels of the government and was secretary of the navy under President Fillmore. His *Swallow Barn* was to be found in the sixth-grader's reader.

That same volume contained *The Raven* by Edgar Allan Poe. There was also *The Gentle Hand* by Timothy S. Arthur (1809–1885). Arthur was an interesting man who had been literally raised on the streets of Baltimore. He is known best for his magazine articles and novels — such as *Three Years in a Mantrap* and *Ten Nights in a Barroom*.

Questions

1. At the time he wrote the "Star-Spangled Banner," Francis Scott Key actually titled his poem what?

2. In an ad for pantyhose (Slender-alls), what quote from a very famous ex-Baltimorean is used?

3. What did Robert Ripley (of "Believe It or Not" fame) and Mrs. Reuben Ross Holloway (of Baltimore fame) have in common that caused Congress to pass an important piece of legislation in 1931?

4. Name the dancer who once performed on "the Block" and who besides stripping, wrote poetry — sending one poem to President Harry Truman (which he apparently enjoyed).

5. "Boog" Powell was the American League's first MVP in 1970. What is his real first name?

It Could Have Been Worse . . .

Theodore Dreiser became a close friend and sometime companion of H. L. Mencken. Over the years the two men would correspond.

In one letter, Mencken told his friend: "The other day a dog peed on me." He went on to ask Dreiser if he agreed with the notion that this was a bad sign.

Dreiser wrote back to the concerned journalist, and his reply seemed to make sense. "A spirit message informs me," he wrote, "that the dog who offended you now houses the migrated soul of Edgar Allan Poe, who thus retaliates."

Retaliation! What had Dreiser meant?

Mencken knew immediately what his friend was implying. In the past, it had been Mencken's custom to take groups of his drinking buddies to Poe's grave after a heavy night of lifting a few. Once at the grave, he would instruct his chums to urinate on it — explaining that it was a sign of respect.

16

Questions

1. What were the "Bloody Tubs," "Rough Skins," "Red Necks," and the "Bloody Inks?"

2. What was the original sentence handed down to Spiro T. Agnew by Judge Hoffman in 1973 — considering that the vice president had resigned and had pleaded no contest to a charge of income tax evasion and was described in a 40-page document as someone involved in kickbacks, extortion and bribery over a period of ten years?

3. In 1879 two research scientists from Johns Hopkins submitted a paper that has since resulted in the revolution of the American diet. What was the discovery made by Constantine Fahlberg and Ira Remsen?

4. What is the name of the first black Catholic church in the United States?

5. Name the occupation of John T. Bailey who once ran for a seat on the Baltimore City Council from the 4th District and was the author of *Mind Over Meter*.

He Was on the Ball...

George Beam, Baltimore shopkeeper, was the man responsible for bringing baseball to the city in 1859. He called his team the Excelsiors, in honor of the Brooklyn (New York) Excelsiors.

To make sure the team got the best coaching tips, Beam brought Henry Polhemus, a businessman and outfielder for the Brooklyn team, to Baltimore. The ball club played in what is now Druid Hill Park and at Flat Rocks. Today the Druid Hill site is under water.

Some of the other teams that sprang up in Baltimore included: the Orioles, Federal League Terrapins, Pastime, the Marylands, the Lord Baltimores, and the Baltimore Yellow Stockings.

Questions

1. Name the team that represented Baltimore in the Atlantic Division of World Tennis.

2. Name the first TV program done live at the studios of WBAL-TV in the 1950's and featured Rhea Franklin.

3. The Triple Crown of baseball requires that a player have the highest batting average, the most runs batted in, and the most home runs during a season. In 1909 the award went to Ty Cobb. Jimmy Foxx and Chuck Klein shared the award in 1933. Ted Williams won it twice — once in 1942 and again in 1947. What Oriole won the honor in 1966?

4. Who was H. L. Mencken making reference to when he wrote of this man and his untimely death by saying: he had been like "catnip to women?"

5. What famous Broadway musical was actually based on the "good, old days" at Forest Park High School?

Boy, Aren't You Glad He Didn't Live in Baltimore? . . .

Chances are that if author, Bram Stoker hadn't done something that most Baltimoreans love to do, we would never have experienced one of the truly great and often-imitated horror stories of all time.

Well, according to Stoker, he got an idea for a horrifying tale the day after he experienced the worst nightmare of his life. The scary dream had been brought on by a dinner of crabs the evening before. The tale he produced from this crab-induced dream was *Dracula*.

18

Questions

1. Where would you find the tallest object in Maryland?

2. His first wife was Helen Woodford; she was a Texan he had met while she was working as a waitress in a Boston cafe. They were married in a Catholic Church in Elkton, Maryland when he was 19 and she was 17. They remained together for 14 years, adopting a daughter, Dorothy. Helen died a year after leaving him, and after having a nervous breakdown, in a house fire. Who was this former Baltimorean?

3. What were/are "Baltimore Blues?"

4. Name the Morgan State graduate (1961) who became the first black mayor of Philadelphia, Pennsylvania.

5. When the first train arrived in Washington from Baltimore in the 19th century, it was witnessed by what United States president?

But Everyone Does It . . .

During a pretty heavy disagreement with a local police officer in 1969, a truck driver used profanity and received a 30-day stay in jail. It appears that a 320-year-old law, forgotten by most people, was still on the books. This law was used by Magistrate Charles J. Simpson of Westminster to sentence the transgressor.

It appears that the law dated back to the days of George Calvert, the first Lord Baltimore. It called for any conviction of blasphemy to be met with a fine and a jail sentence.

The case was appealed to the circuit court. There Judge Edward Weant, Jr. ruled the law to be unconstitutional. It was his feeling that the law was a violation of freedom of speech. It is an historical fact that the Maryland legislature had repealed the law against cursing in 1953 — but they had left unchanged the statute against blasphemy.

Questions

1. How close was the vote of the United States Supreme Court when it upheld the protest against compulsory prayer in public schools launched by local personality, Madalyn Murray (O'Hare)?

2. The Vagabond Players, founded in 1916 in Baltimore, is the oldest continuous little theater group nationally. Name its first one-act performance.

3. The closest loss in Super Bowl history came in 1971. That day Dallas was beaten by the Colts, 16-13. The only scoring pass for the Colts came during the second quarter. Johnny Unitas threw the ball to his receiver, but that man did not make the score. What did happen in this circus play?

4. Name the Baltimore intellectual who founded the Hadassah movement.

5. Mike Boddicker became a hero in the 1983 World Series. His pitching was compared to the work of Michelangelo by Oriole scout, Jim Russo. It was superior. However, in high school Mike actually played what other position?

A Hypochondriac's Premature Death . . .

The year was 1937. The patient had spent most of his life complaining about one ache or pain after another. The fact that he was a hypochondriac probably delayed the recognition of his real, final illness.

He first lost his sense of smell on the right side. Then he experienced severe headaches and dizzy spells, but he refused a spinal tap that might have revealed his brain tumor. Some friends and admirers noticed that he was stumbling when performing. He suddenly went into a coma and was taken to Cedars of Lebanon Hospital in Los Angeles. Spinal fluid indicated the tumor.

A call for Dr. Walter Dandy, Johns Hopkins Hospital's famous brain surgeon, revealed that he was away sailing on the Chesapeake Bay. By the time he was reached only phone consultation was possible, as a transcontinental flight from Newark, New Jersey would only delay needed surgery.

The Los Angeles doctors began surgery the next day, but five hours afterward the patient was dead. The effects of the operation and the removal of a malignant glioma from the left temporal lobe had been too much. The death of this famous personality and the limitations that prevented the noted surgeon from being present during the operation left the nation stunned.

If Baltimore had been able to supply the much-needed cross-country air service at the time, Dr. Dandy might have been able to save the life of George Gershwin.

20

Questions

1. When the first concert for the public was held in the Joseph Meyerhoff Symphony Hall, it was broadcast over television by the Maryland Center for Public Broadcasting. Who was the TV host for that show?

2. What man, whose name is a household word in Baltimore, became the president of his first business venture by the mere flip of a coin following his 1933 graduation from the University of Maryland Law School?

3. He was buried for a second time in 1875 — 26 years after his first burial. His second grave is only yards from the first, and it has a monument that was paid for by the contributions of school children. Name this fortunate unfortunate.

4. What book by a local author is subtitled: *A Survival Guide for the Bedeviled Male*?

5. Name the Orioles who hit grand-slam homers in consecutive innings.

When Are You Old Enough?...

At one time, it was popular to use the phrase: "to Oslerize." It appeared in newspaper columns, cartoons and letters of the day. The origin of the phrase is credited to a valedictory address delivered at Johns Hopkins University around the turn of the 20th century.

That day, a Canadian physician, Sir William Osler (1849-1919) addressed the throng that had gathered. He is quoted as saying: "My . . . fixed idea is the uselessness of men above sixty years of age, and the incalculable benefit it would be in commercial, political, and in professional life, if as a matter of course, men stopped work at this age.

A popular periodical of the day headlined: "Osler Recommends Chloroform at Sixty."

Questions

1. Who were Mr. Owings and Mr. Renfield?

2. The whipping post figured prominently in the history of justice in many colonies and early states of this nation. Maryland was no exception. In 1809 it was repealed — except for slaves (and that was done away with in 1864). However, it was resurrected in 1882 and was applied to a single crime by the state legislature. Name the crime.

3. How many stars were on the flag that flew over Fort McHenry at the time of the 1814 British attack?

4. What was so unique about the Pimlico Special held on October 29, 1948?

5. Name the Glen Burnie barber who appeared in her "birthday suit" in the July 1979 issue of *Playboy* magazine.

It's Not How You Play the Game . . .

When St. Brigid's and Sacred Heart, both Catholic elementary schools in Baltimore, met in 1958 to play soccer, no one had the slightest idea that they were embarking on a history-making event.

The teams were tied at one game apiece — each team winning their game by a score of 1–0. The third game went to the final seconds with no score by either team. The fourth and decisive game took three days to complete.

On the first day, with the score tied at 1–1, there was a need for four 10-minute overtimes, two 5-minute overtimes, and one 15-minute sudden death period; the game was called for darkness. On the second day the score remained tied and there were two more 5-minute overtimes and one sudden death period.

Finally Pat Brooks scored the winning goal for St. Brigid's. It is possible that never have two teams been so evenly matched — in any sporting event. Think about it.

22

Questions

1. What florist has the distinction of preparing the "black eyed susans" using during the Preakness events at Pimlico? What is so unique about these flowers?

2. At the entrance to the campus of Georgetown University sits a bronze statue of its founder. Name this Baltimorean.

3. During the 1960's the proponents of psychedelic rock felt that through this form of music one could achieve the same mind-bending effects that were available from LSD. Regardless of the success of the music in helping its listeners to achieve the simulated hallucinogenic effects of LSD or not, one of its chief advocates, a Baltimore-born singer, was voted Pop Musician of the Year in 1968. Name him.

4. A student from Harvard was on his way home to visit his parents when he fell between two railway cars in Jersey City, New Jersey. Fortunately, he was rescued by a man who grew up near Baltimore and was on his way to visit his sister in Philadelphia. Incidentally, the rescued student was named Robert and his father lived at 1600 Pennsylvania Avenue in Washington. Who was the rescuer?

5. Many popular words and phrases have popped up during our brief history. One such American word is "hooker." It has been used primarily to describe prostitutes. Two schools of thought have emerged regarding its origin. The one accepted by most historians is that credit goes to General Joseph Hooker who rounded up ladies of the evening in Washington in 1863 and forced them into an area near the Treasury Department. This action, just prior to licensing houses of prostitution, resulted in the area becoming known as Joe Hooker's division and the women being called "hookers." The second school of thought gives Baltimore credit for the origin of the word. Explain.

At Least It Wasn't a Shotgun Marriage . . .

Typically, June has been a popular month for weddings. Atypically, one June wedding in Baltimore was not very "typical." On June 9, 1823, the Reverend John Cannon of Baltimore joined in marriage Mr. William August Gun and Miss Emily Maria Pistol of Petersburg, Virginia.

Questions

1. Prior to making their modern debut in Baltimore, where were the Orioles located, what was their name, and what colors were their uniforms?

2. For what railroad did the legendary John Henry work?

3. What does "Baltimore" mean in Irish?

4. In what 1951 Academy Award winning film does a female from Baltimore help a starving young painter by purchasing his art?

5. In what significant wartime event did the cruiser *U.S.S. Baltimore* participate?

History in the "Making"...

On Saturday, February 23, 1861 Joseph Howard, a reporter for the *New York Times,* sent a dispatch from Harrisburg, Pennsylvania that made history. Howard had been assigned to report the events surrounding the move from Springfield, Illinois to Washington, D.C. by the Lincoln family — following the presidential election.

In Harrisburg, word of an assassination plot circulated. A respected source revealed the plot to the new president. Howard's dispatch read:

> "Statesmen laid the plan, bankers endorsed it, and adventurers were to carry it into effect."

Supposedly, one plot called for Lincoln's train to be derailed and the passengers slain. If this failed, the next plan called for men to surround the carriage that was to carry Lincoln from one Baltimore depot to another and assassinate him with pistol and dagger.

According to the story, Lincoln was spirited away at 9 p.m. on a special train, wearing a Scotch plaid cap and a long military cloak to make him unrecognizable. The party passed safely through Baltimore at 3:30 a.m. and reached Washington at 6 a.m. Upon arrival in the capital, Allan Pinkerton sent a coded message to Harrisburg that read: "Plums Delivered Nuts Safely."

Numerous books have shown drawings of this event and it has become part of Lincoln lore. The plot was real. But, because Howard had been prevented from participating in the fateful journey by a detective hired to protect Lincoln, the disguise portion of the story was created to add flavor to the important events. The story was a hit. The *Times* sold out. Other illustrated newspapers picked up the dispatch and printed their own versions of Lincoln's trip through Baltimore. As Howard would later say, "The story was absolutely correct, the trimmings were pure imagination." So, remember the next time you see one of those drawings of this fateful event — it didn't happen that way.

Questions

1. Baltimore has always been a popular place to hold a political convention. Name the party whose 1840 convention pitted the likes of Martin van Buren against William Henry Harrison. Who won the nomination?

2. Following his resignation in February 1984 as general manager of the Colts, what NFL team did Ernie Accorsi join?

3. David Murdock, California multimillionaire, invested both time and money in a project to rescue portions of Howard Street. When a mysterious fire swept through the vacant Hecht Department Store in early 1983, the city was assured that the project would continue as planned. One of Murdock's spokespeople went before TV cameras to calm fears that the project would be pulled out. He was a well-known individual who had been convicted of perjury and conspiracy, as well as obstruction of justice in the Watergate incident under Richard Nixon. Name him.

4. With whom did stripper Blaze Starr claim to have had a fleeting rendezvous in a closet in a New Orleans hotel in 1960?

5. What was *The Constellation Question*?

Just Wait Long Enough and the Weather Will Change . . .

Maxwell Anderson's play "Elizabeth the Queen" needed revision. When it opened in Philadelphia with Alfred Lunt and Lynn Fontanne in 1930, it was a disaster. It was hoped that when the play came to Baltimore it would take off.

However, the weather in Baltimore was more promising than the play — and the weather was bad. Torrential rains poured down on the cast as they arrived for rehearsals. Since Anderson had not produced the rewrites the play needed in the past, there was little hope that he would come up with them now. Things did not look good for the Baltimore run.

When Anderson showed up the day after their arrival in town with the precious rewrites, confessing that he had discovered an inspiration, the cast was exhilarated. As a result of the play's success, Anderson returned to his Rockland County, New York home and made sure he remained inspired. On top of the roof above his studio, Anderson had a sprinkler system installed. It appears that he had been inspired by the sound of the rain hitting the windows of his Baltimore hotel and he wanted to make sure that anytime he needed future inspiration, all he had to do was turn on the sound of rain.

Questions

1. Name the Baltimorean who was the pioneer of the drive-through gas station and the "visible" gas pump.

2. How did Confederate Hill at Loudon Park Cemetery get its name?

3. The jockey who has won more money than any other professional in racing was Willie Shoemaker. His earnings amounted to $79,672,384 at the end of 1980 and included 7,923 victories. However, he won the Preakness only twice. Name his mounts on those two occasions.

4. Odgen Nash, Baltimore's famous poet-wit, was a regular on what CBS television show of the 1950's?

5. The first presidential radio broadcast was made in June of 1922 from Baltimore. Name the president who made this historic broadcast and the event that was the focal point of the day.

Without a Trace . . .

On August 18, 1930 Van-Lear Black, the key figure in the growth and rehabilitation of the *Sunpapers* of Baltimore, flew to Newport, Rhode Island from New York. The purpose of his visit was to be with his daughter. She had recently made him a grandfather — delivering twins.

Later, Black returned to New York aboard his yacht, Sabalo (which had been used on frequent East Coast cruises with friends, such as Franklin Roosevelt). Following dinner along the New Jersey coast, Black went out on deck for a smoke and disappeared. The yacht was searched from top to bottom with no trace. A Coast Guard search was useless. Nothing came of a Navy search. And finally, airplanes ordered out by Governor Roosevelt were unsuccessful. Black was a good swimmer. But no trace was ever found of the Baltimorean.

26

Questions

1. The crossing of Charles and Baltimore streets was given a special name by an ordinance of the City Council, signed by Mayor E. Clay Timmanus on December 12, 1906. What is the name of the topographical center of Baltimore?

2. "Baltimore Oriole" was published in 1942 and later used in the 1944 film "To Have and Have Not." Who wrote this song?

3. He once said: "One does not have to go to college to be able to select fertile fields. All one needs is what my grandmother called gumption, my father called horse sense and most people call common sense. Some people have it; some don't." What remarkable man and investment giant (who never worked a day on Wall Street) said this?

4. What are bugeyes and pungies?

5. Frederick Douglass, the famous black abolitionist, once worked as a ship's carpenter in Fells Point. Where did he get his last name?

The Sport of Kings . . .

War Admiral was a supposedly invincible horse. The owner of Seabiscuit felt that the big male could be beaten. Fans of the sport of racing hoped that the contest would be put together. The world wanted to see the two horses race against each other.

However, when the opportunity presented itself on Memorial Day 1938 at Belmont Park, Seabiscuit withdrew.

The next opportunity came on November 1, 1938 at Pimlico. There were no other starters in the race — called the Pimlico Special. The 1³/₁₆ mile race was run in 1 minute and 56.3 seconds. Seabiscuit defeated War Admiral by four lengths and won the purse of $15,000. Technically, this was not a match race.

Questions

1. Who was the Orioles' manager when they won the 1966 American League title?

2. Bob Lind was a Baltimore-born, Chicago-raised song writer. He was a devout fan of Bob Dylan and tended to write with a folk-oriented style. In 1966 he made the national charts with what composition?

3. Following the great fire of 1904, what president's daughter visited Baltimore to express the wishes of her father and the nation?

4. The first live TV broadcast from Baltimore was done on October 30, 1947 by WMAR-TV. What was the location?

5. Carl Schmidt was substituted for an injured friend in a sporting event in Middle River in 1983. The 21-year-old not only outplayed all others present that day; he set an unbelievable record. Name the sport.

But Could He Act . . .

Jack Dempsey and Red Grange both appeared in motion pictures in the 1920's. But they weren't the only sports legends to appear in the new fad — so did the Babe. Baltimore's own George Herman Ruth made a quickee entitled "The Babe Comes Home" (which also appeared as "Headin' Home"). It was filmed in Fort Lee, New Jersey so that Ruth could dash across the Hudson River and play ball in the afternoons. When one says that the film was a "quickee," they weren't kidding; actual shooting time was only a few days.

One day, after missing batting practice and showing up with make-up still on his face, Yankee manager, Miller Huggins barked at him, "What are you, a movie actor or a ball player?"

When Babe received his check for his acting, he did something rather out of character. Rather than spending the money on a fast time with booze or women, Ruth promptly put the check in his wallet and forgot to cash it. He did show it to his friends from time to time, but the fact is, Ruth never cashed the check for $25,000.

When months had passed and George finally went to a bank to cash his earnings, he received a shock rather than money. It seems that the film was what might be modestly called a failure. The film company went bust and the check bounced.

28

Questions

1. On July 4, 1960, a new 50-star flag was unfurled for the first time anywhere in the world — over Fort McHenry. What was the special occasion?
2. Who was Hoggie Unglebower?
3. Tamara Dobson of Baltimore studied acting at the suggestion of Sidney Poitier. What was the movie in which she first appeared for Warner Brothers?
4. Where was Baltimore's first commercial passenger airport located?
5. Henrico Caucici was paid $7,500 for his efforts on what Baltimore attraction that weighs thirty-six tons?

Just as Good as a Set of Fingerprints . . .

On June 21, 1838 William Stewart met his father, Benjamin; the two went off to visit one of the older Stewart's properties in Baltimore. Impatient to inherit his father's wealth, William had made plans to obtain the money sooner than nature had intended.

As the old man climbed a hill and walked toward his property, the son raised a previously hidden pistol and shot his father several times. The man died instantly. To conceal the deed and make identity of the victim difficult, the boy proceeded to obliterate the face by smashing it with a hatchet.

Impatience, not with greed but with the murder plan, does William in. The clerk who sold William the hatchet told police that he recalled selling the weapon; he also remembered that his customer did not want it wrapped because, as he was told, it was going to be used soon.

In addition to the testimony of the store clerk, Baltimore police made use of a more important piece of data. They used the pistol balls taken from the dead man. Through scientific study, it was proven that William's pistol was the weapon used in the fatal shooting. This was the very first time in United States history that ballistics were employed in pinpointing a killer. Stewart was found guilty and sentenced to a long prison term.

Questions

1. On December 28, 1983, a truck loaded with musical instruments and equipment headed for a performance at Radio City Music Hall in New York City was highjacked at a Baltimore truck stop (in Woodlawn). Although found the next day in the city, for a time the loss of the $300,000 worth of instruments had what recording star quite upset?

2. Who gave the city the land upon which was built the Baltimore Museum of Art?

3. What was Holden Smith's reaction to being cut from the 1983 Colt football team roster?

4. On Christmas Eve 1898, a Baltimore-made product was anonymously sent to Harry Cornish, the athletic director of the Knickerbocker Club in New York City. The gift resulted in the death of Cornish's housekeeper. What was the product involved in this most bizarre 19th century murder plot?

5. Today one can buy books that tell us "how to" do literally anything: How to Live Longer, How to Buy Real Estate, How to Get a Better Job. What was the "how to" book written by George Herman Ruth?

Oops! . . .

On December 24, 1873, a black servant of one of Baltimore's wealthiest and prominent residents ran to the offices of the *Sun* to tell of his master's death. Adolph Schuch, the watchman on duty at the offices that cold night, turned the man away. No one was at the *Sun* building; the offices had been closed early due to the holiday.

What was to be done with the note the servant had been given by Dr. Alan P. Smith? The physician had wanted the paper notified of the sudden death. Was there another possibility?

Wandering about, the servant spied activity across the street. He approached the people and asked them if they could help. Could they help? What a question to ask a competitor? The unfortunate news was welcomed by the people at the *American* and the next day, the competing newspaper scooped the *Sun* in telling the public of the death of Johns Hopkins.

30

Questions

1. Name the Monday column written by H. L. Mencken for *The Evening Sun* that became his single greatest source of fame.

2. What were Brills, Peter Witts and Birneys?

3. Charles Hopkins, a merchant from East Baltimore, opened fire on a group of people in April of 1976. Three shots were fired and one person — a city councilman — was killed. Hopkins was found innocent by reason of insanity and sent to a mental institution. Who was the councilman killed?

4. Johnny Unitas set a record by throwing one or more touchdowns in 47 consecutive games. The uncomparable hero accomplished this feat over a span of more than three seasons. Who were his three favorite receivers during that period?

5. On Wednesday, October 3, 1849 a letter was sent to Dr. J. E. Snodgrass. It read: "Dear Sir — There is a gentleman, rather worse for wear, at Ryan's 4th ward polls, who goes under the cognomen of _____, and who appears in great distress, & he says he is acquainted with you, and I assure you, he is in need of immediate assistance. Yours, in haste Jos. W. Walker" Who was described in this letter and what were the events that precipitated the letter?

Sight for Sore Eyes . . .

When the North German steamer *Willehad* arrived in the port of Baltimore on February 8, it was refused permission to dock. After all those many days sailing across the Atlantic, the passengers, many of them children, had to wait a bit longer to see their new home.

What a sight! The travelers could not believe their eyes. The city was in ruins.

Refusal to dock was due to the tremendous fire that had ravaged the port city — burning through the business and port districts. On Tuesday, three days after the fire had started, an OK was given for the *Willehad* to dock and discharge its cargo.

Aboard the steamer were 470 passengers — all were emigrants to this country from Europe. And the first sight they had of their new homeland was one of ruin and dying flames and the quarantine quarters in which they were placed that day in 1904.

Questions

1. In the 105th running of the Preakness (1980), some felt the winner had actually bumped the horse that "placed." Who did win? What was the winning jockey's name? And what was so unique about the second-place entry?

2. Name the Baltimorean who successfully argued in the now famous school desegregation case, *Brown vs. Board of Education,* that held that "separate but equal" education was unconstitutional in 1954.

3. When "And Justice for All" was filmed in Baltimore, Al Pacino played the young lawyer and John Forsythe was the bad guy. Who played the gun-toting judge who sat on the window ledge outside his office?

4. What was the phrase burned into the infield grass at Memorial Stadium on one July night in 1980 prior to a weekend series which pitted the Orioles against the Boston Red Sox?

5. Who was once the head mistress of Bryn Mawr School and was also known as a classicist and author of *Mythology* and *The Greek Way*?

And You Thought She Could Only Sing . . .

Discovered by Baltimore's own Chick Webb, Ella Fitzgerald appeared in four motion pictures. They were: "Ride 'Em Cowboy" filmed in 1942, "Pete Kelly's Blues" made in 1955 with Jack Webb of "Dragnet" fame, the 1958 movie "St. Louis Blues," and "Let No Man Write My Epitaph" filmed in 1960.

Questions

1. What was the name of Baltimore's first mayor?

2. In the TV series "Edge of Night," what was the name of the Baltimore actress who once portrayed a character, Poppy Johnson?

3. Before the Baltimore Blast moved to town, they were where? What was their name?

4. What company advertises: "Sleep like a kitten?"

5. After leaving professional football, what other sport did Big Daddy Lipscomb take up?

The Defense and the Prosecution Were Both Wrong . . .

"Inherit the Wind" was one of the most popular films made in the 1960's. The Hollywood version of the 1925 Scopes' "Monkey Trial" had Spencer Tracy playing Clarence Darrow opposite Fredric March's William Jennings Bryan. The cantankerous reporter from Baltimore, H. L. Mencken, was played by Gene Kelly. Mencken had gone to Dayton, Tennessee to report on the events surrounding the trial of the rural school teacher.

During the movie, the protagonists join forces to denounce Mencken, telling him: "Where will your loneliness lead you? No one will come to your funeral!" What did occur when Mencken died years later was partially under his control; the rest was not.

On January 28, 1956 Mencken rested on a sofa in his row home at 1524 Hollins Street. The sounds of "Die Meistersinger," his favorite opera, filled the study as operas often did when he listened to the Saturday broadcasts from the Metropolitan Opera House on the radio. A friend joined him and his brother, August, for dinner that evening. After conversation — conversation impaired by faltering speech brought on by his 1948 stroke — Henry retired. Some time during the night he quietly died of a coronary occlusion.

Because of his own instructions, a few close friends met at the neighborhood funeral home. He had specifically requested that no ceremony of any kind be held. Darrow and Bryan had been wrong.

After cremation at Loudon Park Cemetery, Mencken's ashes were buried next to those of his wife, Sara.

Questions

1. When burlesque was king on "the Block," many well known personalities played Baltimore: Phil Silvers, Jackie Gleason, Sophie Tucker, and Milton Berle to name a few. Another performer headlined on "the Block" named Cliff Edwards. By what stage name was he known?

2. What was the connection between Reggie Jackson and former City Councilman, Donald Hammen?

3. During World War II, Japanese soldiers commonly yelled what insult at American GI's that included a United States president, a former Baltimorean, and a country singer?

4. Name the ship that Francis Scott Key was aboard when he wrote the poem that became known as "The Star-Spangled Banner."

5. What is the name of the local singing group that became the first Baltimore group to sign a contract with a national recording company?

Nobody's Perfect . . .

President James Madison married a widow named Dolley Payne Todd. She had a son, who on her wedding night, insisted on sleeping with his mother and new stepfather. The boy continued to join them each and every night throughout their honeymoon. It appeared early on that the boy would present a problem in the life of Mr. Madison.

Beneath the social facade of life in Washington and in the White House (so named by Dolley, who tired of it being called the President's Palace), there loomed the presence of the small boy. Night after night, he continued to insist on sleeping in his mother's bed. He grew more troublesome in adolescence, becoming more of a challenge to his parents. Dolley was often embarrassed by her son, who, from an early age, tended to loaf around his stepfather's stables. At one social function, the lad pulled the wig off the head of General Van Courtland. What was the answer? Could someone or some place be found to help in handling the boy?

What about a good school? Two were tried. Alexandria Academy, founded by George Washington, proved a failure. Saint Mary's Academy in Baltimore came close. At Saint Mary's the boy met his match in one Father Dubourg, a non-nonsense priest who was successful in disciplining him for the first time in his life. Graduation came in 1812, but he refused to go to Princeton and was eventually sent to France on a diplomatic adventure. There the delinquent got into trouble over an affair with a Russian countess and ended up in a debtor's prison.

Questions

1. The first practical submarine was designed and built by Simon Lake at the Columbia Iron Works and Drydock Company in Baltimore in 1897. What was the "H. G. Wellsian" name of this vessel?

2. John Eager Howard gave a tract of land to the city that ran west and north of the center of town and was named for an American Revolutionary battlefield. Name the tract of land.

3. In "Diner," there is a scene where the boys go to a club to watch a stripper in action. After their big night out, they go to what local eatery and are surprised to find the stripper there drinking coffee?

4. In 1979 the United States Postal Service issued four stamps honoring American architecture. What Baltimore landmark was portrayed on one?

5. Where would one look to find the grave of presidential assassin, John Wilkes Booth?

He Was Not Easily Impressed . . .

Harry Truman wrote to his wife Bess on August 23, 1935 about Senator Millard Tydings of Maryland:

> "It is now 10:00 P.M. and the Senate is considering the Flood Control Bill and the sarcastic and cynical Senator from Maryland is making a speech against it. Huey (Long) and (Homer T.) Bone and most everyone are trying to make him look ridiculous and without success. Tydings has a most peculiar complex. He's a most selfish and egotistical person. I don't know which is more insincere, Tydings or Huey. I urged Huey to jump him about the ship subsidy, a bill Tydings is for, one of the worst pieces of graft in the history of the country. But Tydings I think was attorney for a banking outfit, interested in starting a ship line from Baltimore to several European ports by having Uncle Sam pay the bill. The government spent some six or seven millions on the project, and Mr. Morgan and Kermit Roosevelt seem to have been the only ones who made a profit. I don't like him. He's not on the level. But he's having a good time and the galleries are laughing. He's even pulverized Huey, which is something even if he is wrong. We'll pass the bill anyway."

Questions

1. Name the important "Southern song" with a borrowed tune that was initially a verse written by a Baltimore professor teaching in a Louisiana college in 1861 and considered by many to be subversive.

2. Named as the Best of "Baltimore's Best" in February of 1982, Dr. Steven E. Kopits was once the Chief of Pediatric Orthopedics at Johns Hopkins Hospital. He is today the director of what organization?

3. Lee Bonner heads up a Baltimore-based group that makes commercials such as the one that featured Bob Turk — "You've Got Sunshine on a Cloudy Day" weather commercial. Name the feature length film that Bonner worked on entirely in Baltimore.

4. Jim "Catfish" Hunter had only one 20-game season with the New York Yankees. Actually, in 1975 he won 23 games and lost 14. Who was the losing pitcher in Hunter's 20th victory that year?

5. According to historical records, what current resident of Baltimore fired the final shot of World War II?

Too Much Can Cause Cavities . . .

In November of 1976 free agents hit the market in baseball. Back in December of 1975, arbitrator Peter Seitz ruled in favor of two pitchers who had played that year without contracts: Andy Messersmith of the Los Angeles Dodgers and Dave McNally a former Oriole, then with the Expos.

The two pitchers felt, as did many other players, that a player was owned by a team for the length of his contract plus one year — the option year — but no longer. The team owners, however, took the position that the option year was self-renewing, under conditions of the reserve clause.

McNally lent his name to the case and retired. Messersmith was signed to a lucrative contract by the Atlanta Braves. Well, in 1976 the Orioles found themselves losing Reggie Jackson (who had been picked up in a trade with Oakland) to the likes of George Steinbrenner. Jackson went to the Yankees for a reported $3 million. At the time, Ken Holtzman (former teammate with the "A's" and the "O's,") remarked that Jackson said the year he arrived in New York, that a candy bar would one day be named after him. He was right!

36

Questions

1. Who was the one-time riveter at the Glenn L. Martin Company who invented the aluminum ski?

2. In 1933 Goucher College presented Edgar Allan Poe's only play. Name it.

3. To gather data for his book, *The Professional Amateur,* what author practiced as quarterback with the Detroit Lions and the Baltimore Colts?

4. In April of 1978 a poorly organized and very confused "pot party" was held in Wyman Park by local Yippies. What was the formal name of the party held?

5. Abraham Lincoln's funeral train stopped in Baltimore and over 10,000 citizens viewed his remains. Where was this viewing held?

Fact or Fiction . . .

Lazaretto Light served as a Baltimore city landmark for more than 125 years. It sat on what was once called Gorsuch Point. Because an isolation hospital was built on the point, the name Lazaretto stuck — especially since the hospital dealt with smallpox victims primarily. The lighthouse that was constructed was 34 feet high and made of brick.

Lazaretto Light figured in a hoax thought to have been perpetrated by a young man who had come to Baltimore in 1831 — the same year the Light had been constructed. This stranger spread the rumor that a man was going to attempt a stupendous feat or stunt on the first day of the forthcoming month. On that day this man would fly the 2½ miles from the Light to the Shot Tower. This was unheard of.

On the day set for the feat, a large crowd gathered to watch. As the time drew near for the event to take place, individuals in the crowd began to bet on the possibility of success or failure. However, the time for the feat came and went. No flying man was spotted. Then it was determined that a joke had been perpetrated on the city; it was the first day of the month, all right — the first of April — April Fools Day.

Who was responsible for the joke? What was his reason for constructing such a plot? Well, the perpetrator really pulled one over on his fellow citizens. But he had gathered a good deal of data for an unfinished story he was writing. The events and the Lazaretto Light gave him the stuff he needed to complete "*The Lighthouse.*" And so it was that Edgar Allan Poe had done some research prior to completing his story.

Questions

1. Besides "The Babe Comes Home" (also known as "Headin' Home") made in 1920, what two other movies did Babe Ruth appear in?

2. What was the *President Warfield* and how did it change history following World War II?

3. The words to "The Star-Spangled Banner" were those of Francis Scott Key, but the tune was not his. What was the title of this popular tune of the day?

4. Built in 1899, the Colosseum was located at Harford Road and Herring Run. It drew crowds as large as 2,000 to watch what sport?

5. Name the eating and drinking establishments that were opened or owned by Bill Pellington, Johnny Unitas, Art Donovan, and Ordell Brasse.

Give Me Strength . . .

During the Whig national convention, held in Baltimore in 1852, spirits were very high. In addition to the high hopes of party supporters, large quantities of alcoholic beverages were consumed — so it is fair to state that "spirits were very high." Often raucous and always lively, the convention was wrought with dissension. Members seemed to argue over the slightest point or issue.

When a local minister was invited to the convention hall to deliver a prayer to the delegates, they broke into instantaneous debate over when the prayer should be delivered. Finally, after much argument, the prayer was omitted altogether.

38

Questions

1. What player in the North Atlantic Soccer League (NASL) holds the record as the only player to stay with a single team during his entire career?

2. During what was known as the Assay Period, what made Baltimore so unique among all cities in the nation?

3. What was the largest list of nominees for the Preakness ever received?

4. Ed Flanders portrayed Dan and Doug Watson played the role of Phil. This made-for-TV movie gave insight into the anti-war movement in this country brought on by our involvement in Vietnam. Name it.

5. The first home of the Baltimore Museum of Art was located where?

Who Made a Monkey Out of . . .

When H. L. Mencken described the Scopes trial to readers of the *American Mercury* in 1925, he said it was "the greatest since that held before Pilate." Mencken, who was known as the high priest of irreverence, practiced his trade whenever and wherever he saw fit.

After listening to the preachers of Dayton, Tennessee, and with an appearance of sympathy, he once replied: "Oh well, I have always said I would be converted to any religion for a cigar and baptized in it for a box of them."

After the trial ended and responding to the news that William Jennings Bryan had just died (three days after the trial), Mencken said: "God aimed at Darrow, missed him, and hit Bryan. But our loss is Heaven's gain." Poor Bryan! He had defended Scopes and lost. And a brief three days later, Bryan was dead. Another loss. Mencken just could not let the opportunity pass without comment.

Questions

1. National Basketball Association records indicate that a player who once suited up for Syracuse, Philadelphia and Baltimore between October 31, 1954 and November 4, 1965 holds the record for the most consecutive games played in a lifetime — 844. Name this player.

2. Where can you see the largest private art collection in Baltimore?

3. The Parker Estate was obtained by the city and turned into what?

4. Who did Baltimore Mayor, Donald Schaefer, "marry" in 1983?

5. Moe Drabowsky ("Mischievous Moe") was a right-handed pitcher with the Orioles in 1966 through 1968 and then again in 1970. He set what record during the 1966 World Series?

Well !!!!...

Russell Baker, a former Baltimorean and local reporter — later of the *New York Times,* once wrote:

> "Baltimore is permissiveness. The pleasures of the flesh, the table, the bottle, and the purse are tolerated with a civilized understanding of the subtleties of moral questions that have been perfectly comprehensible to Edwardian Londoners. Gross and overt indulgence, however, is frowned upon. The gunned corpses that litter New Jersey are not part of Baltimore life. That sort of thing is vice. Vice leads to cruelty and suffering, and what's more, is in bad taste. Sin is something else. Baltimore tolerates sin."

40

Questions

1. Requested to make the first acceptance speech in American political history, what man said in his acceptance letter that he was unable to reconcile an appearance with his "sense of delicacy and propriety?"

2. On November 16, 1918, Rosa Ponselle became the first American-born singer to debut at the Metropolitan Opera with what distinction? Can you name her first role or the opera in which she first appeared?

3. Who is described in the following: he began playing baseball in 1918 for the "A's" and later replaced Connie Mack in 1951 upon Mack's retirement; he managed the White Sox for 13 years and put time in as the manager for Baltimore, Cincinnati, Detroit, and Cleveland?

4. Name the 1969 Alfred Hitchcock film (his 51st feature) that was based upon a novel by Baltimorean Leon Uris.

5. What was the eventual destiny of the ruler who granted the Calverts their charter for Maryland?

And the Legend Goes On and On . . .

Legend holds (and it is merely legend with no historical support) that Betsy Ross made the first American flag. The story should actually be credited to her grandson who began spreading the version 30 years after her death. According to him, Elizabeth Griscom Ross — known to us as Betsy — was visited by a secret committee in June of 1776, including George Washington, and asked to put together a flag for the new nation. It is a great story, but there is no historical evidence to back up the tale. It is a fact that the original flag was the design of Francis Hopkins of New Jersey — a lawyer, author, artist, and member of the Second Continental Congress.

On the other hand, the Baltimore flag story is factual and the evidence is substantial. Mary Pickersgill did make the flag that flew over Fort McHenry during the British attack in 1814. It was actually sewn at Claggett's Brewery due to its huge size. It was made of four hundred yards of first quality, long-fibered English wool bunting (only because the desired material was not made in the United States at that time). The flag had 15 stars, 8 red stripes and 7 white stripes. And because we have the actual bill preserved for us, we know that the flag cost $405.90.

Questions

1. In what unfortunate way did Henry Gunther of Baltimore enter the history books?

2. Yes, local poet and wit Ogden Nash wrote the "Candy is dandy, but liquor is quicker." But where was it first published?

3. Which is older: the *Constellation* in Baltimore or the *Constitution* in Boston?

4. In what year did the Colts first experience wins of a double digit figure?

5. Name the attraction in Canton that was once cited by Ripley's "Believe It Or Not" as the "smallest park in the world."

I Didn't Hear Anything, Did You? . . .

In 1930, someone planted a bomb on the back porch of Baltimore's Mayor Broening. When the bomb exploded, it blew up half of the house. Very fortunately, no one was injured.

There were two prominent theories: the police felt that the work was that of an anarchist (Baltimore did have individuals who were linked to violence and the city did attract speakers who favored anarchy, such as Emma Goldman — considered by many as "the most dangerous woman in America").

Local anti-Prohibitionists had a different idea. They thought that the explosion was actually the result of a private still blowing up. Many people felt that Broening had one in his house.

Questions

1. Name the horse that won the first Triple Crown.

2. What Baltimore mayor committed suicide while in office?

3. On July 4, 1828, President John Quincy Adams turned the first shovel of earth to begin construction of the C & O Canal. The canal was intended to link the Potomac River with the Shenandoah and Ohio river valleys. On the same day, another monumental event was taking place in Baltimore. Name it.

4. Name the former coach of the University of Miami's national championship football team who was once the head coach of the Colts.

5. Obtained in 1702 by James Carroll, this property had been abandoned by its first settler, a Quaker named Charles Gorsuch. Carroll called the area Whetstone. What is found on the same site today?

But I Didn't Know What I Was Doing...

Sometimes, if you look hard enough, you can find a Baltimore connection to almost anything. Try this one on for size.

Today you can visit the Armed Forces Medical Museum at Walter Reed Army Medical Center and see, protected behind plexiglass, the shattered leg of a military hero — Dan Sickles. Sickles lost his leg in the Wheat Field at Gettysburg to a cannonball; amputation saved his life. However, years earlier it was something stranger that saved his life and is the focus of this story.

Dan married 17-year-old Theresa Bagiolo. She, in turn, met Philip Barton Key — son of Francis Scott Key ("The Star-Spangled Banner") — and an affair began. The affair grew day-by-day and threatened the marriage. Key took an apartment just a block from the Sickles' home in Washington, so that he could be close to his new love.

One day, an anonymous note was sent to Congressman Sickles, telling of the affair. When confronted, Theresa confessed. But nothing changed. Finally, on a Sunday in 1859, Dan saw the lover's signal that meant the coast was clear. The frustrated husband ran to the love nest and found them together. Key ran to the street, pursued by Sickles who drew a pistol, shouting, "You have dishonored my house! You must die!" Two shots rang out and Key fell dead.

Sickles was tried and released on strange new grounds. He defended himself by stating that he was "temporarily insane." The plea worked and is the first such example in United States legal history. By the way, the Sickles' marriage was dissolved.

Questions

1. In the life of Babe Ruth, who was Brother Mathias?

2. Baltimore City College opened its doors in 1839 under what other name?

3. There have been only a few 99-yard touchdown pass plays in NFL history. The first was in 1939 (Washington Redskins), while two others were thrown by the Redskins. The fourth was thrown against the Colts in 1966. Who was responsible for this?

4. Among the fine collections of the Smithsonian is an 1820 pillar-and-scroll shelf clock made by Seth Thomas, the famous clock maker of the 19th century. There is also a very rare 1810 clock that was made by black craftsman, Peter Hill. However, the oldest clock made in America was produced by what resident of the Baltimore area?

5. While living in Arizona, Jim Palmer was offered a basketball scholarship by what university?

The Final Curtain . . .

The James Adams Floating Theatre was, for a long time, the only floating theater on the Atlantic coast. Officially, the name of the huge barge-like craft was the "Playhouse." This is how she was listed in the register of American merchant vessels. Home port for the Playhouse was Baltimore, Maryland.

Built in 1914 in North Carolina, the theater seated up to 700, had 8 bed-dressing rooms, a 19-foot stage, and a dining room. Although she was powerless, she was towed around her circuit from one port to another. A former circus performer, James Adams, ran the operation with the help of his wife. Adams' younger sister, Beulah, was known as the "Mary Pickford of the Chesapeake."

One of the most exciting events in the life of the Playhouse was the 1924 visit of Edna Ferber who spent a week on the barge collecting material for her novel, *Show Boat*. When it was finally made into a motion picture, the Times Theatre in Baltimore showed the film during the last Baltimore appearance of the barge in 1939. The curtain fell on the life of the James Adams Floating Theatre on November 14, 1941, when fire destroyed it on the Savannah River, Georgia.

Questions

1. What was unique about Baltimorean Charles Randolph Uncles?

2. Baltimore was the first city in the world to accomplish this feat. Paris had the same luxury 12 years later, becoming the first European city to make the claim. What was this accomplishment?

3. In the history of football, where would you find the name of Andrea Mann listed?

4. The first rehabilitation school for disabled American war veterans was established in 1921 in Baltimore. Where?

5. What highly visible Baltimorean had the Washington Press Club in stitches in 1976 when she confessed that some people on Capitol Hill had mistaken her for Carl Albert in drag?

The Butler Did It . . .

The Pinkerton Detective Agency was quite fortunate to hire a young, middle-class Maryland high school dropout. He brought what might be called a good deal of native ability to the job. He became a good detective and put a number of experiences under his belt while employed with the Baltimore office. For example, he successfully tracked down and arrested a man who had made off with a Ferris wheel; he shadowed the mobster, Nick Arnstein; and worked — although unsuccessfully — to clear film star Fatty Arbuckle in the famous rape case that ruined the actor's career.

During World War II, Sam, as he was called by his friends, contracted tuberculosis and found it impossible to continue his work with the agency. Inspired by the success of ex-detectives Allan and Frank Pinkerton — both having turned to writing — Sam began to write detective stories that were based on his own exploits. His style was dramatically different than any other writer of such works. His characters, many of whom were based upon friends and acquaintances, were tough-talking, hard-bitten, hard-drinking, low-lifes — unlike himself.

He and Erle Stanley Gardner were the most popular writers for the pulp magazine "*Black Mask*" which published most of his stories. However, it was the creation of Sam Spade that really brought him the recognition he sought. Spade eventually made it to the silver screen in the film "The Maltese Falcon," starring Humphrey Bogart. And so it was that Samuel Dashiell Hammett, the former dropout from Maryland and one-time Baltimore detective, finally found his true love and became one of the most popular writers in America.

Questions

1. Name the Baltimore original: inexpensive to produce and merely a toy — although many who purchased it felt it was much, much more. It was a fad in the 1920's and its most important piece was made of wood. It can still be purchased today.

2. In 1844 the first "dark-horse" presidential candidate was nominated in Baltimore. Name this man and the party that sent him on to the White House.

3. What 1958 John Barth novel was made into a 1970 film starring Stacy Keach (as the catatonic hero) and featured James Earl Jones and James Coco?

4. In 1860 Abe Lincoln remarked: "What kills a skunk is the publicity it gives itself." More than a century later, what Baltimore personality told reporters: "You don't get into a pissing contest with a skunk?"

5. Lenny Ripps, former Baltimorean and head of comedy for Walt Disney Productions, was head writer for what ill-fated TV series that involved two young advertising copy writers?

Maybe He Should Have Answered His Fan Mail . . .

F. Scott Fitzgerald spent parts of his life living and writing in Baltimore. Some of that time he spent waiting for his wife, Zelda, to be released from treatment for mental disorders.

Fitzgerald had fans wherever he went. One fan began writing to him, but never received a single note in return. This fan also wrote to other writers she respected for their contributions to contemporary literature. But none of these individuals returned the compliment either. As time went by she felt her already pronounced inferiority complex swell even more.

She saw herself as a writer and attempted short stories of the Jazz Age. She submitted a few to "Smart Set," a magazine of some reputation, edited by H. L. Mencken. Her stories were rejected. In 1926, she began a novel but abandoned the idea when the hero began to resemble an old boyfriend. She decided to leave the Jazz Age in the hands of Fitzgerald. However, she did not give up totally.

Finally Margaret Mitchell, the fan, wrote *Gone With The Wind* — not just another "short story." Her idol Fitzgerald felt it had none of the elements that make literature — especially "no new examination into human emotion." When the novel became a movie, David O. Selznick hired professional writers to work on the script. One writer wrote: "I was absolutely forbidden to use any words except those of Margaret Mitchell; that is, when new phrases had to be invented, one had to thumb through and check phrases of hers that would cover the situation." The screen writer was F. Scott Fitzgerald!

Questions

1. What was the name of the women's pro basketball team from the Baltimore area in 1979?

2. Norman Lear had six different TV shows running on prime time during 1975 and 1976. Among them were: "All In The Family," "Maude," "Good Times," "The Jeffersons," "Sanford and Son," and what other comedy?

3. "Baby Ruth," as much as some would like to believe, was not named after Babe Ruth. In fact, the candy bar was named for the daughter of President and Mrs. Grover Cleveland. However, the Babe did try to market his own candy bar. What was its name and what was its success?

4. What is found carved in relief on the grave monument of Edgar Allan Poe?

5. Complete this ad for a Baltimore-made product of 1895: "If You Keep Late Hours For Society's Sake, _____Will Cure Your Headache."

The Other Side of the Street . . .

Some interesting stories have come out about "the Block" — one of Baltimore's most notorious attractions. Sam Lampe's Two O'Clock Club once featured Roberta Jonay, a dancer who had become the protégé of Mrs. Franklin D. Roosevelt. When Jonay appeared at the club, Lampe sent a letter to the White House with a special invitation to the first lady to attend her performance. In a very polite note, Mrs. Roosevelt's secretary replied to Lampe that "her engagements prevent her going to Baltimore. She regrets not being able to accept your kind invitation." That sure would have been a first!

In another example of life on "the Block," Julius "Lord" Salsbury, a small-time hood, was hired by the Cohen brothers at The Oasis. He bought the brothers out eventually, got the club back on its feet, and later sold it to the Spina sisters — better known as Pam Gail and Jackie Lamont. Salsbury, for various reasons, found himself under investigation by the FBI. One night, while his apartment at the Horizon House on Calvert Street was being watched by agents, Salsbury disappeared — never to be seen on "the Block" or in Baltimore again.

Questions

1. Name the Baltimorean who assisted Robert Peary in 1886 on his first exploration of the far north and was with Peary when the North Pole was reached in 1909. In addition, what was this assistant's true role in the 1909 adventure?

2. How did banker, James McCulloch, create a situation that led to a major United States Supreme Court decision in 1819?

3. Three decades before his cousin, Wallis Warfield Simpson, married her good friend and one-time King of England, Edward VIII, what Baltimore author was writing novels of social protest?

4. Name the 23-year-old, ROTC-trained officer who led his men into combat in Vietnam and was decorated and eventually became a Baltimore Oriole.

5. Fillies have done well in numerous runnings of the Preakness. How many can you place as winners or second-place finishers in: 1903? 1906? 1915? 1924? and 1980?

You Know Where to Find Me . . .

Even the most respected or the wealthiest of people run into problems from time to time. However, when law or customs restrict an individual's ability, it is sometimes extremely difficult to overcome some problems. Charles Carroll of Carrollton is an interesting example.

Carroll was prohibited by law from holding public office in Maryland because he was a Roman Catholic. Catholics, in fact, could not teach the young or practice law at the time. Carroll, the only Catholic to sign the Declaration of Independence, was born to great wealth in Annapolis. He was raised to believe that all men deserved the right to practice their beliefs and had the responsiblity to preserve the rights of others.

His career as a public servant — and eventual patriot — began in 1733, when he wrote a series of articles which denounced government decrees with no legislative action. When he finally got an opportunity to show his mettle in 1776, he did so with style. Carroll signed the Declaration of Independence, but his signature was not enough. So that the British would know where to find him if they wanted to hang him as a traitor, Carroll placed his address next to his signature.

48

Questions

1. What was Abraham Lincoln's reaction to the April 19, 1861 riot that followed the stoning of Union soldiers by pro-Southern residents in Baltimore and the death of 4 soldiers and 13 civilians?

2. Name this man: 5-foot, 7-inch Princeton graduate who was said to dress up in women's clothes, who joined the army in 1917 — but left to write verse for street car ads, who married the daughter of the chief justice of the Alabama Supreme Court, and later admitted her to Sheppard-Pratt Hospital.

3. Who was the only professional baseball player ever thrown out of a game for praying?

4. The *Patrick Henry* was the first of its type built at the Bethlehem-Fairfield shipyards. What type of ship was she?

5. What were "Fizz Water" and "Chevy Chase?"

I Didn't Know That . . .

Dorothy Lamour, Hollywood actress, once had a cosmetics manufacturing plant on Falls Road at Rockland Mill with her husband William Howard.

The last gas street lamp was put out in 1957.

Dr. Elmer Verner McCollum (1879-1967), professor of biochemistry at Johns Hopkins, discovered vitamins A and D.

The first electric streetcar in the U.S. ran from Oak Street (now Howard) and 25th to Roland and 40th in 1885.

The last passenger train left the Mount Royal station, now a part of the Maryland Institute, in 1961.

American Turf Register and Sporting Magazine was the first sports magazine ever published in the United States — and it was published right here in Baltimore by John Stuart Skinner. The first 56-page issue hit the streets in September 1829, and it obviously dealt with horses.

The *Evening Sun* reported a train wreck to its readers because the news had been delivered to the paper by an airplane hired to gather the information. This is the first example of an airplane being used for any news-gathering purpose by a newspaper. The year was 1920. Just two days after it reported the train wreck, the Canadian Curtiss biplane located a submarine in trouble off the Delaware Capes.

Questions

1. What was the nickname of the Colt who fell on fellow player, Gino Marchetti, and broke Gino's ankle in a 1958 game against the Giants?

2. The Maryland Institute for Emergency Medicine, known to many as "Shock Trauma," located at the University of Maryland Hospital, is the premiere medical facility of its kind in the entire nation. It was the brainchild of what man?

3. Name the local personality whose trademark has been a folded dollar bill — folded into the initials of the individual who is given the bill as a gift.

4. What symbol appeared above the B & O's initials in the B & O Railroad Company's logo.

5. Traditionally, what is sent by Pimlico management to the barn of the Preakness winner?

Sloppy, Sloppy . . .

In 1843 Adam Horn, alias Andrew Hellman, was a man already known to police as the murderer of at least one wife. Horn, a very, very sloppy slayer, chopped up his second wife, Malinda, in their home. Although he buried most of her parts in a nearby apple orchard, Horn forgot to take all parts with him. The unburied remains were discovered in full view, lying about the house. Horn was captured, tried, found guilty of the crime and executed.

Another Baltimore murderer was salesman G. Edward Grammer. In love with another woman, Grammer decided to kill his wife — rather than seek a divorce. With a rather heavy instrument, Grammer bashed in his wife's head. Her body was placed in their automobile and a fake accident was created. Police investigators were not convinced of an "accident" — especially when they discovered a rock placed on the accelerator. This was not an uncommon practice; the device was used to cause a driverless car to keep moving. Under grilling, Grammer admitted the crime. However, during the trial that followed, he recanted his earlier confession, pleading "not guilty." Not convinced, the jury found the evidence and premeditation clear. Grammer was convicted and condemned. On June 11, 1954 he was hanged at the Maryland Penitentiary.

Questions

1. What was the medical breakthrough made by Dr. Helen Brooke Taussig, a pediatrician associated with Johns Hopkins?

2. In 1830 the Baltimore and Ohio Railroad was on the verge of bankruptcy, even before the fledgling company was under full steam (so to speak). The problem that seemed so unsurmountable centered on a severe curve that was forcing the Railroad's main line to be laid with a radius of only 150 feet. What solution finally solved the problem?

3. With whom did Earl Weaver compete in tomato-growing contests?

4. What was so unique about the Baltimore Ravens basketball team?

5. Jake Kilrain made sports history on July 8, 1889 in Richburg, Mississippi. He later returned to Baltimore to live out his life as a local celebrity and bartender. What did he do?

Things That Go Bump in the Night . . .

For centuries it was not always easy to be sure that a certain percentage of individuals buried around the world were, in fact, dead. Comas and other situations that lowered body temperatures and practically halted functions could make it difficult or impossible to be definite about the occurrence of death. And considering that large numbers of bodies were not embalmed, this only added to the concern.

Well, do not let it be said that Baltimore wasn't progressive when it came to this area. Christian Eisenbrandt of the city designed the earliest known "life signal" device to be patented in the United States in 1843. This device was described as a "life-preserving coffin in case of doubtful death." It was unique from other coffins in that it had a spring-assisted lid that would enable the person inside to open the lid — so long as the coffin remained above ground.

Questions

1. Johns Hopkins Hospital has buildings that were built as the direct results of financial gifts from benefactors for whom the buildings are today named. Who was the financial supporter for whom the "Brady" Urological Institute is named?

2. In November of 1973, a press release from the office of the mayor called a certain landfill the world's prettiest and it was known that this Highlandtown dump was to be a prototype for future landfill operations in Baltimore. However, a decade later, a team from Princeton University declared that the site had been illegally used to dump chemical waste and that there had been coverups. However, the landfill, which closed in 1980, offered no significant health risks. What was its name?

3. Name the great competitor who died in 1967, was known as "The Gray Ghost," and won 21 of 22 starts, including the 1953 Preakness, before retirement.

4. What military hero captured abolitionist John Brown and spent three years working in Baltimore before going to West Point as its superintendent?

5. Architect Robert Mills designed three. The smallest is in Baltimore. The largest is in Washington, D.C. The middle one stands in Boston. What did he design?

Can We See into the Future? . . .

There are many recorded examples of people who had the ability (some say luck) to predict the future. For example, Byron Somes, a reporter for the *Boston Globe,* dreamed one night of the eruption of Krakatoa. He set his dream down on paper the next morning for the newspaper — with no real proof of its occurrence. The eruption did occur in 1833, just as Somes had dreamed. The explosion on the Indonesian island was felt as far away as Texas.

Well, Edgar Allan Poe seems to have had this strange ability. A short story, *The Narrative of A. Gordon Pym,* was written by Poe just after leaving Baltimore. The story may have been influenced by his stay in the port city. It told of three survivors of a shipwreck who were floating adrift in an open boat and, because of hunger, killed and ate the young cabin boy who was with them. His name was Richard Parker. Strange as it may seem, about 50 years later, three survivors of an actual shipwreck actually killed and ate a cabin boy. His name was Richard Parker.

52

Questions

1. What song is played as horses are led to the starting gate prior to the start of the Preakness each May?

2. The Baltimore Colts played in Super Bowls III and V. They won one game and lost the other. In both games, the winning scores were identical. Which game did the Colts win — the 1969 game or the 1971? What was that winning score?

3. On March 1, 1954 five Congressmen were wounded by three Puerto Rican Nationalists as the members of the House of Representatives were working on the floor of the House chamber. They included Clifford Davis, a Democrat from Tennessee; Alvin M. Bentley, a Michigan Republican; Kenneth A. Roberts, a Democrat from Alabama; and Benjamin F. Jensen, a Republican from Iowa. Who was the Maryland Democrat shot that day?

4. P. T. Barnum (1810-1891) had quite a collection of human oddities that he showed off in the cities of the world. There was Josephine Clofullia — the Bearded Lady, and the Wild Man of Borneo. The Feejee Mermaid was actually one Joyce Heth, and there were Eng and Chang — the famous Siamese Twins. What role did James Murphy, Jr. of Fells Point assume in the Barnum menagerie?

5. What was the connection between Baltimore showman, theater owner and hospital benefactor, James L. Kernan, and a professional dancer, Catherine Devine?

It May Be Chile, but It Sure Is Hot . . .

Under orders from the president of the United States, the cruiser *Baltimore* (the same ship that would make history seven years later as part of Admiral Dewey's squadron in the Battle of Manila Bay in 1898) was sent into the harbor of Valparaiso, Chile. As has often been the case, the American visitors were not welcome. On October 16, 1891, a mob of angry anti-American demonstrators attacked members of the ship's crew who were on shore leave — killing 2 and injuring 17. President Harrison was able to finally get a $75,000 indemnity from the government of Chile.

Questions

1. Pat Hayden was the first winner of football's "Punt, Pass and Kick" contest to play pro ball. What Colt also won the contest?

2. The American Revolutionary Army felt that the news media of this country had become too leftist and too liberal by the early 1970's. They decided to do something about it and took action. A victim was selected and taken prisoner. His tape-recorded voice was sent to his employer and said in part: "I have been kidnapped by the American Revolutionary Armies. I wish you would first tell Virginia and the children that I am all right, that I have been treated with courtesy and that I have not been abused." Who was speaking on the tape?

3. When Lyndon B. Johnson made his first stop in the 1964 presidential campaign, he appeared at what Baltimore location?

4. Ginger Rogers won the Academy Award for Best Actress in 1940 for a serious performance as a white-collar girl whose baby dies. The film was adapted from a novel by Baltimorean Christopher Morley. Name this RKO film.

5. Name the United States president who described Mayor William Donald Schaefer as his "favorite mayor" in the country.

A Lot of Money for Those Days . . .

Baltimore got its first excursion boat as early as 1813. And on Sunday, June 13 the locally-built steamboat, *Chesapeake*, under the direction of Captain Edward Trippe (who owned one third of the vessel) made its first trip to Annapolis. The boat was 137 feet long, 21 feet wide and weighed 183 tons plus. It had a single deck and one mast. A 10-foot-diameter paddle wheel propelled the *Chesapeake*. When she sailed out of port on that June day at 8 a.m. the charge was $1 each way. For $2 — a lot of money in 1813 — one could sail round trip from Bowley's Wharf to Annapolis.

Unfortunately, within a few months travel was hampered by the threat of British attacks on Annapolis and the surrounding area. The *Chesapeake* was really hampered by the eventual attack on Baltimore in September. After the end of the War of 1812, the steamer remained the only ship of its kind in the Baltimore-Annapolis area until 1815. In June of 1820 she fell on hard times and broke up.

54

Questions

1. Name the two switch-hitters for the Orioles who hit 30 or more homers in a single season.

2. John Dos Passos died at his home at Cross Keys on September 28, 1970. What world leader died the same day?

3. Name the organization which sponsored the "Columbiad" to the moon in Jules Verne's novel *From the Earth to the Moon* and organized themselves to change the earth's surface in the sequel, *The Purchase of the North Pole*.

4. Each year the Mystery Writers of America give an award for the year's best mystery novel. It is the equivalent to the British Gold Dagger Award. What is it called?

5. Garry Moore got his radio start in Baltimore at WBAL. He was the one responsible for the discovery of Carol Burnett and three TV quiz shows. Name them.

Even Fillmore Would Have Liked the Honor . . .

When one looks over the unimpressive record of Millard Fillmore, it is difficult to come up with something that makes his tenure as United States president the least bit interesting. However, with the help of a well-meaning journalist, even Millard had his moment in the sun.

A young H. L. Mencken, then writing for the New York *Evening Mail*, put together an article in honor of the 75th anniversary of the bathtub in America. The title of his article was "A Neglected Anniversary." And according to Mencken, Americans did not take favorably to the idea of regular bodily bathing. In fact, he wrote that it took a brave individual — like the president of the United States — to take the politically dangerous step of having a tub placed in the White House. Millard Fillmore was just the man.

According to the article, even Fillmore's staff objected to the radical move. But, undaunted and with blazing strength, Fillmore started a trend toward the eventual acceptance of the bathtub nationally. The myth had been started. A new piece of American trivia had been created. Mencken denied that the story was fabricated — until 1926, when he felt compelled to write a retraction.

But this, coupled with another retraction written a few years later, did not quell the public's belief in the myth. Even President Harry Truman told vistors to the White House of Fillmore's contribution. Near the time of his death, Mencken was offered two cases of Labatt's ale a month for the rest of his life in exchange for the rights to the story. Mencken accepted the offer made by a Canadian film producer.

Questions

1. When quarterback George Shaw was hurt in a 1966 game against the Chicago Bears, what Pittsburgh Steeler reject replaced him?

2. Some people feel that "scrod" has its origins in New England. Others think it has origins in Baltimore. What does "scrod" mean?

3. To whom do we give credit for the quote: "And this be our Motto, in God is Our Trust."

4. Who was responsible for Babe Ruth's nickname?

5. BWI (Baltimore-Washington International) was the replacement for Friendship International Airport. What field did Friendship supersede?

Two Baltimore Failures in One Lifetime Is Enough . . .

John Bankhead Magruder graduated from West Point at age 20. He was bright and handsome. He met and wooed Henrietta von Rapf, the daughter of a successful Baltimore merchant. The marriage was stormy to say the least.

Magruder's military career boomed in 1847 as his marriage began to suffer from his excessive lifestyle. His reckless attitude won him glory in Mexican combat, but an argument over a card game with a brigadier general would return to haunt him. Magruder always contended that the argument had led to a near-duel. Dueling was the gentlemanly way to settle disputes. "Prince John," as he was known to his friends, selected Thomas J. Jackson (later known as "Stonewall") as his second. However, the duel never came off. Why it didn't has never been clear.

In 1852 the Democratic convention in Baltimore nominated Franklin Pierce, the former brigadier, as their presidential candidate. Charges arose that Pierce had refused to duel with Magruder because he was a coward. Pierce said that he had not been slapped and challenged, therefore no duel was warranted. Pierce won out. And Magruder's histrionics at the convention only made him look like a fool.

On top of this loss, Henrietta, fed up with her life, took their children and sailed for Italy in 1853 — never to see him again. With his second loss under his belt, John went on to fight other losing battles. He fought under Robert E. Lee during the Civil War and later fought for Emperor Maximilian in Mexico. He died alone and forgotten in Houston in 1871, after lecturing for years on the Pierce incident.

56

Questions

1. In 1945 Arthur Laurent's first Broadway play opened. It was a war drama, pitting psychiatry against the partial paralysis and loss of speech of a Jewish GI. In 1949 Stanley Kramer made the movie version, substituting a black for the Jewish soldier. What Baltimore creation lent itself to the title of Laurent's play *and* what was the title of the play?

2. When Edward R. Murrow interviewed the Duke and Duchess of Windsor on his famous TV program of the 1950's, "Person to Person," what game did the ex-Baltimorean play on a coffee table in the living room, while the Duke looked on bravely?

3. Just prior to attacking Baltimore in 1814, what had the British been doing?

4. One of the most important inventions in the history of the world was given its first practical demonstration on May 27, 1844. Baltimore played a key role in the day's events. However, it was actually a man by the name of Joseph Henry who deserves credit for the invention mistakenly given to a one-time artist. Name the invention.

5. There have only been three in baseball history. The second time it was accomplished, Baltimore completed the feat against Louisville on September 7, 1896. What was the feat?

Baltimore Has Always Had Someone with a Comment on Any Subject . . .

"I prefer to forget both pairs of glasses and pass my declining years saluting strange women and grandfather clocks." — Ogden Nash

"She had once been a Catholic, but discovering that priests were infinitely more attentive when she was in the process of losing or regaining faith in Mother Church, she maintained an enchantingly wavering attitude." — F. Scott Fitzgerald

"He has made three separate careers. He began as a biologist, switched to journalism, and then to literature, and finally set up shop as a prophet. My guess is that he'd have been a happier fellow, and much more useful to his nation and his time, if he had stuck by his first choice." — H. L. Mencken talking about writer, H. G. Wells

Questions

1. What political position did Spiro T. Agnew first hold in Baltimore County?

2. In the NFL, Baltimore holds the record for either the most *or* the fewest penalties in one season. Which is it and what is the number?

3. Name the artificial island constructed across from Fort Armistead in 1850 under the command of a future head of West Point and pro-Southern military leader. In addition, name the man.

4. Name the Oriole to become Baltimore's first Rookie of the Year.

5. Ruth Wayne was a veteran performer at the Two O'Clock Club on "the Block." She gained a degree of fame when she publicly sought to win the affection of what European leader?

Talk About Strong School Ties . . .

When John Wilkes Booth attended the Catholic school, Saint Timothy's Hall in Catonsville, he made some friends that he called upon in later life. One of those boyhood friends was Samuel Arnold from Hookstown, Maryland. Arnold at age 30 met with Booth at Barnum's Hotel in Baltimore to plan for the kidnapping of Abraham Lincoln and eventually, his murder.

Another friend from Booth's youth, Michael O'Laughlin, was an ex-Confederate soldier who was recruited for the plot. He and Arnold had been sought out by Booth to help plan and pull off an unbelievable kidnapping. Basically, the plot was this: kidnap Lincoln, hold him prisoner, and ransom him back to the Union in exchange for Confederate prisoners. However, the plan never really got off the ground. On March 14, 1865, an attempt to grab the president was aborted at the last minute. Both Arnold and O'Laughlin returned to Baltimore, rather than going into Washington to attend the last performance Booth would ever make at Ford's Theatre on March 18. Arnold even went so far as to tell Booth, "I have ceased with you."

Booth went off to New York and Boston to probably raise money to be used on a future plot. When he returned to Washington, Robert E. Lee had surrendered to Grant, and Booth had to change his plans.

After the death of Lincoln, Arnold and O'Laughlin were captured, tried and imprisoned. O'Laughlin died at Fort Jefferson, Florida of yellow fever in 1867. Arnold was later pardoned for his efforts in helping Dr. Samuel Mudd in fighting the fever at the fort in 1869. Arnold died in 1906. But just before he died, he told Dr. Mudd that he was never involved in the murder plot.

58

Questions

1. Name the Baltimorean who died on March 18, 1984 and was once the Chairman of the Civil Rights Commission known to many as the "101st Senator."

2. What Baltimore-born composer wrote "I'm Just Wild About Harry?"

3. Baltimore was "the gastronomical center of the universe" according to what famous jurist?

4. This former Pennsylvanian attended Radcliffe and studied psychology under William James. She undertook experiments in brain anatomy at Johns Hopkins University but flunked out. She collected the works of Picasso and was a close friend of Ernest Hemingway. Name her.

5. In 1847, the Baltimore *Sun* announced to its readers that it had made special arrangements for all important and newsworthy items to reach them within 36 hours of any mail delivery by a more reliable source. What was this faster and soon-to-be legendary means?

Statistics About the Renaissance City ...

A 12-year study published in 1981 by Johns Hopkins University indicated that men have a much better chance of living longer if they are married. Sixty percent of those men studied, between 55 and 74 who had lost their wives and those married, had a chance of dying sooner if they were unmarried. The statistics for women are practically the same — either single or married.

In 1976 the Commission on the Review of the National Policy Toward Gambling found that the odds of being arrested in a gambling raid in Baltimore are 747 to 1.

In 1969 hundreds of dead ducks dropped on the streets without any explanation.

The first Ph.D. awarded in the United States came from Johns Hopkins University.

Who were Seth Hockett Ellis and Samuel T. Nicholson? Well, they may rank among the biggest losers of all political times. They were the nominees for president and vice president of the United States on the Union Reform Party ticket. At the party's first convention, held in Baltimore, on September 3, 1900, these men felt like they could whip anyone. But, when they ran against William McKinley that fall, McKinley garnered 7,200,000 votes. Ellis' total was less than 6,000 votes.

Questions

1. Born in Griffin, Georgia, the son of a major in the Confederate Army, he was sent to Baltimore to study dentistry. After two years at the Baltimore Dental College, he returned to Atlanta to take postgraduate courses. Seeking a new life and possibilities of good business, he traveled west. However, he is today remembered as one of the deadliest shots with a six-gun ever seen. Who was this personality who died from the complications of tuberculosis?

2. Red Smith, famous sports writer and social commentator, wrote the following about what baseball player: "When he was fifteen and good enough to become a professional, no scouts from organized baseball knocked at his door. A bid from the Bacharach Giants was more than he expected. After that, it was the Baltimore Elite Giants and winter ball in Latin America, and it was a good life. _____ never asked for more until Branch Rickey offered more."

3. Kenneth Brown, a 30-year-old advertising salesman, became the first victim of something that made its appearance in Baltimore on March 15, 1983. What?

4. During the attack on Fort McHenry by the British in 1814, how many Americans died?

5. Name the Johns Hopkins University graduate and former member of the glee club who won a Nobel Prize in 1919.

It's Hard to Keep Them Around When They Don't Want to Stay . . .

On March 14, 1808, sixteen men overpowered their jailers, killed one in the process, broke down the door of the old Baltimore jail, and made good their escape. Four were recaptured and hanged for the guard's murder. The remaining twelve were never seen again.

On December 6, 1835, ten inmates of the old Baltimore jail pounced on their guards, tied them up and smashed down a door, escaping to freedom.

In 1951, a convict at the Maryland State Penitentiary by the name of Joe Homes spent months digging a twenty-six-foot tunnel from his cell to the outer wall. He made use of iron scraps taken from the prison workshop. Once he hit the streets of Baltimore, Joe Homes was never seen again.

60

Questions

1. Nominated for the presidency of the United States in Baltimore, what man, born in 1782, was the first elected president to be born after the American Revolution — and therefore the first one born a citizen of the United States?

2. Name the recording star who was raised in Baltimore, made it big, and was rumored to have died in 1974 by choking to death on a ham sandwich.

3. Against what team did Cal Ripken, Jr. hit his first career grand-slam home run?

4. After he had become famous for the creation of Sam Spade, what other detective was made popular by Dashiell Hammett — popular in novels and later in movies?

5. During World War II, what role did the *Frigate Constellation* serve?

The Sun *Newsboy Band Excursion . . .*

One of the most popular excursion boats to sail out of Baltimore in the early 1900's was the *Three Rivers*. Built in 1910 at Sparrows Point for some $125,000 by the Maryland Steel Company, the boat was originally constructed to carry passengers on the Potomac River.

On July 3, 1924 it loaded up for a trip on the Chesapeake. Among the numerous passengers were 59 members of the *Sun* Newsboy Band who were planning to participate in the annual Chesapeake Bay Workboat Championship Races on July 4. While off Cove Point, a fire broke out on the saloon deck. Most of the passengers were asleep when the alarm was given, but the majority made it to the decks. Many got into life preservers and jumped overboard into the dark waters. Some got into lifeboats.

Later, when a head count was taken, five of the Newsboys were missing. A search revealed the bodies in the charred remains of the ship's hulk. Spencer D. Hall, captain of the *Three Rivers,* was experienced and cleared of any responsibility. The boys' bodies were buried together at Loudon Park Cemetery.

Questions

1. Name the man arrested for reckless driving and taken to police headquarters in Washington, D. C. and known to have hit a woman with his one-horse shay and fleeing the scene just one year after being nominated by his party in their political convention in Baltimore. NOTE: He was president of the United States at the time!

2. What members of the Orioles became affectionately named "Moe, Larry and Curly?"

3. Who portrayed the role of the desk clerk, Bill, in Lanford Wilson's "Hot l Baltimore" when it opened on Broadway in 1973?

4. What was the first name given to what is now Baltimore's Inner Harbor?

5. During the Civil War, what function did Fort McHenry serve?

Right Name — Wrong Reason . . .

In 1978, Charles Mathias, Jr., Senator from Maryland, wrote to Willard R. Espy in New York and explained that unlike Massachusetts and Virginia, Maryland was not a "Commonwealth." Maryland was, he told him, the "Free State of Maryland" because of its "highly vocal opposition" to the Volstead Act. The Volstead Act of 1919 was an unpopular piece of legislation that went into effect in 1920; the Act plus the prohibition amendment made wartime prohibition permanent.

As Mathias went on to point out, many people would have preferred that Maryland had earned its title as the result of its early practice of religious tolerance or for its early practice of asserting the right of women's suffrage.

Questions

1. Name the one-time Colt who had the most passes intercepted in his career — 277.

2. In Baltimore's financial history, what were paper coins?

3. Identify the local landmark that has changed hands some 18 times — once even before its construction was completed and was officially opened in 1903.

4. Just prior to coming to Baltimore to live, Edgar Allan Poe was expelled from what well-known educational institution for refusing to attend classes for several weeks *and* for making a public appearance stark naked?

5. Where was WFBR radio disc jockey, Johnny Walker, married — in front of an estimated crowd of 12,000.

Eyewitness to History in the Making . . .

William Worthington Goldsborough was a Southern patriot, a military leader, and a Confederate hero. He was also the author of perhaps the best historical work produced on a Maryland unit in the Civil War: *The Maryland Line in the Confederate States Army.*

Born in 1831 in Frederick County, Goldsborough ran away to fight in the Mexican War. In 1850, he went to work for a Baltimore newspaper, after learning the printing trade. He joined a local militia company in 1857 and participated in the mopping-up operations following the raid by John Brown on Harper's Ferry. By May of 1861, he had enlisted in what was to become Company A of the 1st Maryland Regiment and saw action at First Manassas. Later he participated in Stonewall Jackson's valley campaign.

One of the most amazing coincidences of the Civil War took place during the battle at Front Royal, Virginia on May 23, 1862. During the fighting, William actually captured his own brother, Charles. He sent his prisoner to the rear with other federal soldiers. Later, at Second Manassas, William was seriously wounded, and at Gettysburg, he was captured after receiving a bullet wound in a lung.

Following the war, he established the *Times* of Winchester, Virginia. In 1869 he wrote the book on the Maryland Line and published it in Baltimore. The book was ripe with eyewitness accounts. It was a hit and was republished in 1900. Goldsborough died in 1901 from complications during surgery — he refused anesthesia and went into shock on Christmas Day. He was buried in Loudon Park Cemetery with full military honors.

Questions

1. Who became the brother-in-law of "Glorious Betsy" Patterson on Christmas Eve, 1803?

2. In 1968, a rumor circulated around the country that what rock singer — who was raised in Baltimore — was actually the son of Hugh Brannum (better known as "Mr. Greenjeans" on the TV show "Captain Kangaroo")?

3. Name the Baltimore lawyer who graduated in 1960 from Cheltenham High School in suburban Philadelphia — the same school that graduated Reggie Jackson in 1964.

4. What Colt player was injured in a game, hospitalized, released, and returned to the game in time to catch the winning pass?

5. What was the name of the colt who won the first stakes race run at Pimlico in 1870?

C.O.D. Presidency . . .

In 1848, the Whig Party met in Baltimore and nominated Zachary Taylor as their presidential candidate in the upcoming election. A letter was sent to Taylor's home, explaining the party's desire to have him run for the high office. However, a problem arose that almost brought Taylor's race for presidential history to an early end.

At this time in United States history, prepayment of postage on letters and packages was optional. In other words, letters could be sent to anyone in the country and the cost would be paid by the recipient. However, Zach Taylor was not your ordinary letter recipient.

He refused the "collect on delivery" message from his own party. When Taylor's supporters did not get an answer, they figured he was not interested in running. Later, it was learned that the hero of the Mexican War had not accepted the letter because of the cost involved; but it was also learned that he wanted to run for the presidency. Thank goodness for Taylor. That fall he ran in the general election and won — becoming the 12th president of the United States.

It is interesting to note the influence this event had on changing the "collect on delivery" situation with the postal service. In 1855, prepaid postage became mandatory in the United States.

Questions

1. Due largely to the love of what artist's work — by Miss Etta and Dr. Claribel — can the Baltimore Museum of Art boast the world's largest collection of what man?

2. *The City Paper* was originally published under what title?

3. What was the team that the Baltimore Blast played in its first game under their new owner, Nathan Scherr, on February 10, 1984?

4. On February 8, 1934, Francis X. Bushman, the former movie star from Baltimore, obtained a marriage license to marry the sister of what celebrity?

5. When the Pro Bowl was played on January 29, 1984, what was wrong with the helmet of the Colt guard on the American Conference offensive squad?

Not Quite on the Top 40 . . .

Arthur Schwartz was a song writer-composer of recognizable talents. Over the years, he wrote and published numerous songs that were popular in their day. A couple of his tunes have been looked upon as standards and are still played today. Born in 1900, the song writer gained public attention with "I Guess I'll Have To Change My Plans" in 1929. He also composed the popular, "Dancing In The Dark."

However, his first song was one that has been largely forgotten. It is one that almost no one has ever heard. It's not one that we would expect to hear on the top 40. Its title: "Baltimore, Md., That's The Only Doctor For Me."

Questions

1. What is the name of the Baltimore-born authority on polite, socially acceptable behavior and decorum, whose book on the subject was published in 1922?

2. Name the writer and the newspaper he represented, when the following was written: "Baltimore, the team, is a lot like the city. Monotonous. It's like watching nine guys run a lathe. . . The ballpark looks like the Christians and the lions are coming on next. . . Baltimore is going to have to make do with crabcakes as its tourist attraction."

3. What is the actual name given to a copy of a famous statue known throughout Baltimore as "Black Aggie," and where can you find her today?

4. Flag Admiral was entered in the 1983 Preakness and finished 10th in a field of 12. Who was a partner in the ownership of the horse, along with Kentucky breeder, Tom Gentry?

5. What special treatment was given to the flag that flew over Fort McHenry in 1814 during World War II?

The Great Fire of 1904 Was Terrible, but . . .

It is interesting that, considering that so much destruction took place, not one life was lost during the actual fire itself. Rumors did spread that a worker on the docks (in the area now occupied by Harborplace) had jumped into the harbor to avoid the flames and drowned. However, no body was recovered to prove out the story.

James McGlennen did die as a result of the fire — although after it had been put out. He was a Baltimore firefighter who died within days of the fire from pneumonia he contracted while fighting the flames.

There was only one church actually destroyed during the fire. The Church of the Messiah on the northwest corner of Fayette and Gay Streets was consumed. Today the site is a corner of Memorial Plaza.

The bank vault of Hopkins Place Savings Bank was the first to be opened after the fire was extinguished. Once the vault had cooled, the door was removed — after an hour of pulling. The contents were found to be completely unharmed — all $6 million in cash and securities.

Questions

1. It was named by Carolus Linnaeus, the Swedish botanist, who was responsible for instituting the binomial system of nomenclature to classify plants and animals. It's name was derived from a family's colors. What did he name?

2. Three United States presidential candidates attended the March 23, 1983 memorial services for civil rights leader Clarence M. Mitchell, Jr. Name them.

3. What weight is carried by each horse in the Preakness?

4. Walbrook was once considered Baltimore's first suburb and contained some of the city's finest estates. The Johnsons, who owned "Carleton," were also the first family in the United States to own what particular means of transportation?

5. Francis Asbury was made the first bishop of what religious denomination?

It Doesn't Matter How You Spell It . . .

His last name was originally "Bannaky," but it was altered while he was attending Peter Heinrick's Quaker School outside of Baltimore in the 1840's. It would appear, however, that regardless of how his name was spelled, Benjamin Banneker was destined to go down in history.

Andrew Ellicott, a friend of Banneker's, was an interesting fellow. Like his father, Joseph, who loved to tinker and is said to have made the first four-sided clock in the country, Andrew had an interest in mechanics. He devised and tried out a steam-propelled boat in 1789. During a test of the invention, he lost an arm and this prevented him from perfecting his design.

Andrew became a very close friend of Benjamin's over the years, and together they joined Major Pierre L'Enfant, the designer and architect of the national capital. When L'Enfant was dismissed from his position with the government, Ellicott was selected to finish work on the city. History tells us that it was Banneker — the man who invented the first clock in the nation — who memorized L'Enfant's plans and gave them to Ellicott to carry out.

Questions

1. Westminster Graveyard contains the grave of Baltimore's first mayor. Name him.
2. A song was recorded by Bobby Darin about Baltimore. What was it called?
3. Who is recognized as the man who provided baseball with signals used to tell runners and batters what is expected of them by the coaches?
4. During his first term in office, what United States president, nominated in Baltimore, was rumored to have killed his wife about a year and a half after taking office?
5. H. L. Mencken called them "Homo boobiens." According to him, they were people who had done what?

A Sad End for One of Baltimore's Outstanding Visitor-Personalities . . .

In part, her nervous breakdown was brought on by the drinking and carousing of her husband. As early as 1931, she had been diagnosed as schizophrenic; however, her friends felt that her personality had not changed to any noticeable degree.

She was kept as a virtual prisoner by her husband in a Swiss sanitarium. While there, she was unable to send letters to her friends or let them know where she was or when she would leave — so long as he paid the bills. The outstanding fact of the matter is that her so-called mental illness was based almost solely upon the testimony of her husband. He stated that she was prone to hysteria and hallucinations. When one doctor observed that it was the husband who needed emotional treatment more than the wife, he merely dragged her off to another doctor — one that he was able to persuade to commit her once again.

After years of bouncing from one doctor to another and from one hospital to another asylum, she became genuinely mentally ill. One of her stops along the way was the respected facility known as Sheppard-Pratt in Baltimore.

Finally, the pain was over; the sad woman's suffering came to an end. While locked in her room at a sanitarium — the Highland's Mental Hospital, Asheville, North Carolina — on March 10, 1948, she burned to death in a mysterious midnight fire. She could not be identified, due to the fact that the fire completely immolated the body. However, Zelda Fitzgerald was identified by a practically untouched slipper (known to be hers) discovered under her body. Her husband, F. Scott, had died eight years earlier in California, while living with his lover, Sheilah Graham.

Questions

1. Baltimore was dealt a political blow in June of 1856 when the first Democratic convention was held in another city. Six prior conventions had convened in Baltimore, but this year they met in Cincinnati, Ohio. The Whigs did meet in the city that September and supported what candidate and his Know-Nothing ticket?

2. What motion picture was advertised with the following lead: "Suddenly life was more than french fries, gravy and girls."

3. The 47-year-old replacement for Sergiu Commissiona was music director of what orchestra at the time of his selection?

4. What local newspaper was the first to hit upon Robert Irsay's plan to sell the Colts to out-of-town concerns in 1983?

5. Novelist Jon Dos Passos was the screenwriter who worked with S. K. Winston on what 1935 Marlene Dietrich film that was based on the novel, *The Woman the Puppet,* by Pierre Long?

The Man Was Multi-Talented . . .

H. L. Mencken had interests ranging from short stories to novels, from plays to newspaper articles. In 1909, he became increasingly interested in drama. In a short-lived magazine, *Bohemian,* published by his friend Theodore Dreiser, Mencken had his work, "The Artist," printed; it was subtitled "A Drama Without Words."

The same year Mencken published translations of two plays by Ibsen: "A Doll's House" and "Little Eyolf." He collaborated on this project with the Danish consul in Baltimore, Holger Koppel. However, 1909 had still more to offer. Going Back to Dreiser, Mencken sold him two additional short stories for the *Bohemian: The Bald-Headed Man* and *The Psychology of Kissing.*

In 1910, *What You Ought to Know About Your Baby* appeared in the bookstores under the name of Dr. Leonard Hirchberg, a well known Baltimore physician. Mencken was the ghost writer. This was just one more accomplishment for this multi-talented man in less than two years.

Questions

1. Ernie Banks of the Chicago Cubs had his best year for home runs in 1958. He hit 47. However, he set a record in 1955 by hitting five grand-slam home runs in a single season. What Oriole tied that record — for grand-slams — in 1962?

2. Name the former resident of North Avenue and Monroe Street who was a *News-Post* carrier as a boy, who entered World War II at age 17 and later wrote a best-selling novel of the war, who entered City College and flunked English, and was given the key to the city when his war novel was made into a motion picture and premiered in Baltimore.

3. In the Spring of 1981, what lawyer's firm was hired by the parents of John Hinckley to defend their son for shooting President Reagan?

4. What former Colt started the "Shake and Bake Family Fun Center," after being dropped from the team? Who was the Colt coach at the time?

5. Thomas Kensett of Baltimore is credited with perfecting the technique for which all retail supermarkets in the nation today can be thankful. What was his 1850's invention?

A Dead Woman's Legacy . . .

It was winter and the woman entered the medical clinic of Johns Hopkins for an examination. What the doctors found that day in 1951 would change the events in the life of Henrietta Lacks and the lives of researchers for years to come.

The 31-year-old was sick. The cause of her illness was found on her cervix. Henrietta had a small lesion that was found to be malignant. Radiation was used to reduce the size of her tumor, but there seemed to be nothing that could be done. She suffered through eight months of tests and radiation and praying, but time was not on her side and she died.

The surprising thing that has amazed members of the medical community for years was that the cells of the tumor, which had been removed, were found to be alive. In fact, the cells were actually doubling every day. Henrietta had left behind a strong contribution to science at her death. This was the first time that test cells had survived under such artificial conditions. The cancer cells are known as HeLa, and are still sought by cancer researchers.

Questions

1. What group sang "Barefoot in Baltimore?"

2. In 1774, Baltimorean William Goddard organized something to compete with one already in existence and run by the British. What did he start?

3. The Orioles found themselves in a slump during the early days of the 1981 season. In an effort to help his team and himself, the team's third baseman, Doug DeCinces, did something drastic. What did he do *and* what effect did it have during the April 29th game against the Boston Red Sox?

4. The phrase "lost generation" was used by Ernest Hemingway in *The Sun Also Rises* in 1926. Actually, he borrowed the phrase from what former Baltimore resident?

5. In 1979, Towson State University sponsored a series of guest speakers. They included F. Lee Bailey, Yitzhak Rabin, Dick Cavett, and Julian Bond. Name the dynamic duo that started off the series on October 14, speaking on the subject of "Nuclear Energy and Current Events."

Oh, Those Roaring Twenties . . .

The one-time Baltimore graduate of St. Mary's Industrial School could not wait to get out of town and on his own. Baseball was one way out. And, in his own way, as if he was trying to prove F. Scott Fitzgerald correct when he wrote that during the 20's "the universal preoccupation with sex had become a nuisance," Babe Ruth seemed to always be on the prowl.

His old, on-the-road roommate, Ping Bodie, once said that Ruth was always out with women. When asked if he roomed with the Babe, Ping remarked, "I don't room with him. I room with his suitcase."

Periodically, his life style caught up with him. In 1922 he was charged with rape by a girl who claimed he was the father of her baby. Delores Dixon, a teen who worked in a Manhattan department store, told authorities that Ruth had promised her marriage. When he didn't deliver, she hit him with a breach-of-promise suit for $50,000. Ruth called it blackmail; his lawyer called it extortion. The case was settled out of court in 1923.

Questions

1. Name the sports hero who grew up in Baltimore during the days when baseball was played at the Thirty-third Street diamond, and who went on to pro-ball with the Detroit Tigers after graduation from Southern High School and eventually to broadcasting.

2. What event was formerly called the "Monday German?"

3. Describe how the monogram insignia of the Maryland Jockey Club, the oldest in racing, reveals the initials of the organization.

4. Private John Drew, a 28-year-old from Richmond, Virginia, did something at Fort McHenry on November 14, 1880 that no one had done before or since. What did the soldier do?

5. What term did H. L. Mencken introduce to the United States that was in use during World War I in England and was used to describe free and easy women?

Another First for Baltimore . . .

The Orioles won the 1969 pennant by 19 games and finished with 109 wins. That was only three less than the major-league record set in 1954 by the Cleveland Indians. The O's went on to play the "Miracle Mets" in the World Series. During the Series, Earl Weaver gave Baltimore another of its firsts — he was ejected from the fourth game by Umpire Shag Crawford, making him the first manager to be thrown out of a World Series game in 35 years. This game had been held in New York and it was also Crawford's first game of the Series behind the plate. Unfortunately, the Mets won the Series 5–3, scoring 15 runs to Baltimore's 9.

Questions

1. Name the trainer who asked that his remains be buried "at the races" and was interred in the infield at Pimlico.

2. During the Revolutionary War, Martha Washington visited the only period mansion still standing within Baltimore city limits. Name it.

3. After winning the 1983 World Series, what brand of champagne did the Orioles drink to celebrate their victory over Philadelphia?

4. Name him: former Johns Hopkins graduate, tenaciously accused by Richard M. Nixon, federal government official, journalist, Carroll County farmer, who was imprisoned for "pumpkin patch perjury."

5. What local hostelry was once described by Charles Dickens in 1844: "The most comfortable of all hotels in the United States is _____, where the English traveler will find curtains to his bed for the first and probably the last time in America and where he will be likely to have enough water for washing himself, which is not at all a common case."

We Ought to Be in Pictures . . .

Baltimore has figured in motion pictures — in different ways — over the years. In 1983, "The House on Sorority Row" was released by Artists Releasing Corporation. The R-rated movie was directed by Mark Rosman and filmed entirely in Baltimore — "where," as they put it, "nothing is off limits."

Barry Levinson, the writer and director of "Diner," and his wife, Valerie Curtin, appeared in the Burt Reynolds-Goldie Hawn film, "Best Friends."

Local actress, Bess Armstrong, appeared on the cover of *Baltimore Magazine* in December 1981. Karen Allen, of "Animal House" and "Raiders of the Lost Ark," appeared on its November 1978 cover.

A Mickey Mouse cartoon was suppressed in 1932 because it showed a cow resting in a pasture reading a copy of *Three Weeks* by Elinor Glyn — a book considered immoral. Over the years, many controversial films have been considered immoral or pornographic and were banned from college campuses. Among these were "Deep Throat," "The Devil in Miss Jones," and John Waters' (local film maker-director) "Pink Flamingos."

Questions

1. In retirement, one was a Portland, Oregon stock broker, another was the owner of a Philadelphia sporting goods store, still another owned a steak house in Neenah, Wisconsin, and a fourth was an insurance agent in Columbia, Missouri. Who were these people?

2. The John Eager Howard Room at the Belvedere Hotel was originally known as what?

3. Charles Carroll of Carrollton said on July 4, 1828: "I consider this among the most important acts of my life, second only to my signing of the Declaration of Independence, if second even to that." What was he talking about?

4. Stephen Brenner of Dundalk was a personal friend of Eddie Cantor, Bill "Bojangles" Robinson, and Babe Ruth. In 1916 he traveled with "Buffalo Bill's Wild West Show." Name the clown he created in 1908 when he joined Barnum and Bailey's Circus.

5. Name the Baltimore resident who was named on the ballots in both the Illinois and Florida primaries in 1980 as the running mate of independent presidential hopeful John Anderson.

$50 Or $100, It Was an Important Beginning . . .

Historians have not always agreed whether or not the amount won was $50 or $100, but Edgar Allan Poe made an early name for himself in Baltimore in 1833 by entering and winning first prize in a short story contest. *The Saturday Visitor* had offered the prize for the best original short story. The Baltimore publication also offered a prize for the best poem entered. Poe was the original winner for his poem, but could not be awarded first prize in both categories. Winning the award gave Poe an opportunity to also win a new friend — John Pendleton Kennedy. Kennedy was one of the judges in the contest and an individual who helped Poe establish himself as a writer.

While awaiting word of his appointment to West Point, Poe lived with relatives in Baltimore who supported him while writing a volume of verse, *Tamerlane, and Other Poems*. He signed his name Edgar A. Poe on the manuscript which was rare for him. "Tamerlane" was published later in Boston and was a failure. He never forgot his earlier success, however, in the short story contest.

Questions

1. Name the Baltimorean who wrote the script for the Norman Jewison film, "And Justice for All", (Baltimore was the location) that was shot in 1978.

2. What was Ernie Accorsi's counterpart to the Orioles' "Designated Hitters" — the exclusive group that sold tickets within the business community?

3. Name the 1975 Triple Crown winner who had three white legs and a left, front leg that wasn't.

4. Name the graduate of Douglass High School who went on to play the role of Lionel on the TV sitcom "The Jeffersons."

5. The Democrats held their first party convention in 1832 in Baltimore. Who was the man they nominated for president?

The Son of a Baptist Minister and the Actor's Son . . .

Lewis Thornton Powell joined the Confederate Army under the name Lewis Payne. He had the makings of a tough fighter. At Gettysburg, however, he was wounded and taken prisoner. The injured man was sent to Baltimore for care, but escaped after regaining his strength. Running from the federal troops, he ran into and joined the raiding guerrilla rangers of John Singleton Mosby. Not one for a long and questionable fight, he deserted Mosby and slinked back into Baltimore. There he took the oath of allegiance to the federal governement and signed a statement that he would not engage in any activities against the North.

This all may have seemed strange for the son of a Baptist minister from Florida, but his next step was probably even more dangerous. He was recruited by John Wilkes Booth for Booth's plan to kidnap President Abraham Lincoln. And so it was that the minister's son joined forces with an actor's son to commit a crime against the North that would have long-term effects.

The oath that he had taken back in March of 1865 had been an apparent attempt to side step another crime for which he had been arrested — and not a sincere attempt at reconciliation with the government. Back on March 2, Payne had been arrested in the city of Baltimore for the severe beating he had given to a young black girl. He was a devout bigot, and his hatred for blacks had gotten him caught. Eventually, he would die at the hands of the enemy he thought he had fooled — the Yankee government — on a gallows in Washington, D. C.

Questions

1. Name the former Calvert Hall student who went on to study drama at Towson State University and who later was given the role of Murdock on a TV program that the National Coalition on Television Violence named as the bloodiest show on TV in 1983.

2. With his Jungle Band, he cut his first recording in 1929. "Jungle Man" was a cut on one side and "Dog Bottom" was on the flipside. Who was this jazz drummer who had ten years of success before he died of tuberculosis at age 37?

3. Name the winner of the 1967 Preakness *and* the man who presented the Woodlawn vase to the winning horse, jockey and owners.

4. What occupation did Clarence Long have prior to entering Congress?

5. When Elizabeth was born in New York City in 1774, she had no idea that her efforts in starting the first Catholic school in America and a religious order of nuns would one day lead to her canonization in 1974. Who was Elizabeth and what was the name of the Pope who made her a saint?

Yes, This Is Trivial . . .

Twelve-year-old Bud McQuade of Baltimore became the first National Marbles Contest champion in 1922 by defeating seven boys and one girl.

Milton S. Eisenhower spent his 75th birthday with the Baltimore Orioles and more than 500 friends at Memorial Stadium in 1974. He received a lifetime pass to the Orioles' games — in fact to all American League games. The pass was made of 14 karat gold.

The *United States Frigate Constellation* was honored with a song that was published in 1799. The sheet music was titled, "Huzza for the *Constellation*," and sold for $.32 at J. Carr's in Baltimore. It was written to honor her victories over the French.

In 1903, the Baltimore Orioles were dropped to make room for a new franchise — the New York Yankees. In 1954, the Orioles replaced the Browns of Cleveland.

Back on March 25, 1802, Baltimore was the site of the first distribution of free vaccine to the poor. Dr. James Smith produced a smallpox vaccine in a specially built institution in the city and then saw that it got into the hands of the public.

Questions

1. During the 1969 World Series between the Orioles and the Mets, a player was hit on a shoe by a pitched ball. The manager was quick to point out the fact to Umpire Lou DiMuro and shoe polish was found on the ball. The batter was given first base. Who was the batter and what was the outcome of this event?

2. On June 26, 1876, Samuel T. Walcott was killed. Today, a monument stands in his honor at Loudon Park Cemetery — although his body is not there. Where did Walcott die?

3. What United States government post was held by Mayor Robert Milligan McLane in the 1880's?

4. If you are 45 years old or younger and have recently published a book of poems, the Academy of American Poets and the Copernicus Society of America might select you as the winner of $5,000 and what award?

5. In 1983, the subway opened in Baltimore; however, back in 1979 the following slogan was popular among certain people" "I Don't Dig the Subway." Another slogan was: "An Idea Whose Time Has Come . . . And Gone." Who was responsible for these?

You Won't Have Old What's His Name to Kick Around Anymore . . .

In his famous "Checkers Speech" in 1952, Richard Nixon described how he and his wife, Pat, had received a message on the day they were scheduled to leave on a campaign trip. The message from Union Station in Baltimore, said Nixon, regarded a special package that awaited the family and had to be picked up as soon as possible. When the family did pick up their surprise package, it contained a black and white cocker spaniel. It had been sent in a crate from an admirer in Texas who had heard that the Nixon children had wanted a pet. Tricia, then six, named the dog "Checkers."

In 1952, Nixon was running for the vice presidency, and in his now-famous speech, defended himself against charges that he was the beneficiary of a secret political fund. He said at the time, ". . . and you know, the kids, like all kids, loved the dog, and I just want to say this, right now, that regardless of what they say about it, we are going to keep it."

Questions

1. Name the pitcher for the Orioles between 1974 and 1977 who had a father of the same name who pitched for the Chicago White Sox in 1951.

2. For 30 years she refused to remove her G-string when stripping, but was finally convinced in 1977 by an offer of $3,500 per week from the Melody Theater in New York City (at Broadway and 49th Street). Name this Baltimore attraction who finally gave in.

3. What was the title of the first black musical to play on Broadway?

4. In 1872, the first female candidate for president of the United States was nominated; her name was Victoria Woodhull. That year, the first black was nominated for the office of vice president. What former Baltimore resident was so nominated?

5. Who said, "Those who can do. Those who can't teach."

Ex Parte Merryman . . .

On May 25, 1861, John Merryman was taken prisoner by federal troops under command of General Nathaniel P. Banks, the Union commandant in Pennsylvania who was then commanding in Baltimore. Merryman was thought to be responsible for burning a bridge outside of Baltimore in order to protect, in his words, the city and keep troop trains from reaching Baltimore.

The resident of Baltimore was taken into custody and delivered to Fort McHenry for confinement without a warrant and without specific charges. Chief Justice of the United States Roger B. Taney of Taney, Maryland (now known as Taneytown), quickly issued a writ of habeas corpus. However, General George C. Cadwalader, who commanded the fort, refused entry to the United States marshal and ignored the writ he brought with him.

Two days after his arrest, Merryman was the subject of Taney's anger. The justice issued his opinion on the situation and wrote that Abraham Lincoln's suspension of the writ of habeas corpus was illegal (enacted on April 27, 1861 under orders from Lincoln) and no military officers could prosecute civilians otherwise subject to the courts and laws of the United States.

78

Questions

1. What tactic was used successfully against Senator Millard Tydings by his opponent John Marshall Butler, for re-election, in the 1950's that won the support of pro-McCarthy voters?

2. She was born into a family of great influence. Her father had been a governor of the state in 1829, a number of businesses in Baltimore used her skills in public relations, and she went to work for President Lincoln after writing of a plot by a secessionist to capture Washington. Who was this woman who drew up the plan to capture Vicksburg, Mississippi during the Civil War?

3. Name the former anchorwoman for WJZ-TV who once made an appearance on the ABC soap "All My Children." What role did she play?

4. What team did Earl Morrall play for before coming to Baltimore in 1968 *and* where did he go after leaving the Colts?

5. J. Glenn Beall beat him in 1958 by only 7,000 votes for a seat in the United States Senate; J. Harold Grady beat him in 1959 in the primary for mayor of Baltimore. Who was this man?

Tidbits . . .

When Arunah Shepherdson Abell published the first edition of *The Sun* on May 17, 1837, six newspapers already existed in Baltimore.

In 1911, Woodrow Wilson was elected governor of New Jersey; prior to that, he had never held a single public office of any kind. Yet, 22 months afterward, he was elected President of the United States — having been nominated on the 46th ballot of the Democratic Convention held in Baltimore.

It is tradition that horses entered in the Preakness are stabled in Barn E at Pimlico.

Dr. John M. T. Finney (1863-1942) has been called the dean of Maryland's medical professionals. He was the personal physician and surgeon to Mrs. Evalyn Walsh McLean — owner of the Hope Diamond.

In 1969 Earle Monroe was voted Rookie of the Year, playing for the NBA Baltimore Bullets. In 1970 Elvin Hayes of San Diego won the scoring title; however, Wes Unseld of Baltimore was selected as Rookie of the Year and Player of the Year.

Questions

1. The advertising agency of Trahan, Burden and Charles won a 1982 Clio Award for their TV commercial for Schmidt's Blue Ribbon Bread and did so using what 1960's pop song for its theme?

2. "Friendly Fire" was a column written by what person for the "City Paper," while living in what unique location?

3. Name this Oriole: He was in Bluefield, then in Stockton, next came Dallas-Fort Worth, followed by six years in Rochester. Then he went to Columbus, with New York as his last stop — prior to coming to Baltimore.

4. In 1932 he came to Baltimore to appear in a play, "The Last Mile." While in the city, he toured the Maryland Penitentiary to publicize the show. During his stay in Baltimore, he married his first wife, Margaret, and held their wedding reception at Kernan's dining room. Who was this actor?

5. Where does the Preakness Festival Balloon Race begin and end?

What Authors Do Other Authors Read? . . .

In his work, *The Dream of the Golden Mountains,* Malcolm Cowley quoted F. Scott Fitzgerald and described Fitzgerald's wife, Zelda, who was recently home from one of her many visits to asylums. He wrote:

> F. Scott stood in front of Cowley holding his glass and said, "She was the belle of Montgomery, the daughter of the chief justice of the Alabama Supreme Court. We met at the governor's ball. Everybody in Alabama and Georgia knew about her, everybody that counted. She had beauty, talent, family, she could do anything she wanted to do, and she's thrown it all away." Fitzgerald went on to tell the author, "I've been reading him (Karl Marx); Bunny Wilson made me do it. My father belonged to the same Baltimore family as Francis Scott Key. What if they tore down the monument to the author of 'The Star-Spangled Banner' and instead built one for me because I died for communism — a monument to the author of *The Great Gatsby*?"

Questions

1. In 1970 what Colt player was elected president of the fledgling NFL Player's Association and was responsible for the suit that destroyed the Rozelle Rule?

2. Begun in 1804, what is known as the oldest stationer in the Western hemisphere?

3. Legislation was passed and signed in 1902 allowing women to be admitted to the bar. It had been initiated by what woman — who had been the first woman to graduate from the old Baltimore Law School?

4. In what motion picture does the male lead make the following statement: "Look at those Orioles. Baltimore's always been a sneaky town."

5. What monument within the city limits can be found on the seal of Baltimore?

There's Nothing New Under the Sun . . .

Health clubs, spas, working out: so what is really new? Probably nothing. Teddy Roosevelt was the prime example of the athletic male of his day: he boxed, he went on safaris and hunted big game, he lifted weights, he swam, he did things that most men only dreamed of doing.

In Yellow Springs, Pennsylvania, Jenny Lind — known as the Swedish Nightingale — lounged in the mineral waters that were guaranteed to improve her depression and overall health. Such spas were very popular in the 19th century.

Well, Baltimore was not to be outdone. Good health was a major issue in the 1890's and people who had the money joined various clubs that espoused exercise and the pursuit of a healthy body. A Dr. Ralston of the city started the Ralston Health Club. Perhaps this was a risky venture., Perhaps it wasn't; for by 1898, he boasted a membership — nationally — of 800,000. In fact, Ralston was so sure of his health concepts and his ability to merchandise himself that he created and sold his own health food: Ralston's Health Club Breakfast. So popular was his name and his product that he eventually gave his endorsement to a product out of St. Louis, Missouri. By the way, he also gave the product his name. And so it was that the Purina Company and its product, Purina Wheat, became known as Ralston-Purina Wheat.

Questions

1. Hank Peters, the executive vice president and general manager of the Orioles, completed his first full season with the team in what year?

2. What Baltimore landmark was named for: a man born in Ballymena, Ireland, who studied medicine under Benjamin Rush and was a surgeon at Valley Forge, who served as a Maryland delegate to the Continental Convention and Congress, and who was on cabinets for Presidents Washington and John Adams.

3. What Kentucky-bred son of Bold Bidder was owned in part by Harry Meyeroff and ridden in the Preakness by a 19-year-old from Dundalk, Ron Franklin?

4. When H. L., Mencken spoke of a "protein factory," of what was he speaking?

5. In 1978, "Shuffle Along" was revived and expanded from its original size and scope. What was its new title?

Baltimore Girls to the Rescue . . .

General Pierre G. T. Beauregard faced a real problem on July 21, 1861. His troops were engaged in battle at Manassas and suddenly there was reason for major concern. Out of the dust he saw men moving toward him from his left. The question he was faced with was: were these soldiers Federal or Confederate?

Due to the nearly identical colors carried into battle, it was difficult to tell enemies apart. In addition, the uniforms of both armies were quite similar. Spotters could not tell if flags carried by the troops had Stars and Bars on them or Stars and Stripes. Anxiety gave way to fear. Beauregard had been awaiting additional support. Was this it? What if he were wrong?

A sharp breeze caught the flags and they spread open. They had Stars and Bars on them. They were Confederate: Virginians and troops from Louisiana and Mississippi. Revitalized, the Confederates swept through the Federal lines and within an hour, the battle was won. However, Beauregard vowed that such an incident would never happen again. No Confederate soldier would be endangered due to unidentifiable battle flags.

Other officers supported the idea of a new and recognizeable flag. The classic Confederate flag was decided upon: a red field, a blue cross, and white stars. The War Department approved the decision. Eventually, completed flags were presented to the soldiers by Beauregard himself. Those flags had been handmade from dresses belonging to the seamstresses: Hetty and Jennie Cary of Baltimore and their cousin, Constance, of Alexandria, Virginia.

Questions

1. Name the company that owned the moving vans used by Robert Irsay to sneak the Baltimore Colts' equipment from the Owings Mills complex on March 29, 1983. How many were used?

2. It began in 1975, is held each year, and there are heavy penalties assessed against any participant who regurgitates at specific times. What event is being described here?

3. Jacob Fussel became the first person in the United States to manufacture a particular commodity and wholesale it to an eager market in 1851. Name the popular food product he made.

4. When Spiro Agnew ran for governor, what song was borrowed to create his campaign song?

5. Name the individual who was born in the same decade as George Washington, had a running feud with his father for nearly 30 years, had a mother who suffered from a mental disorder, and felt the only way to pay the expenses of waging the American Revolution was to soak the wealthy — which included himself.

Firsts, Firsts, More Baltimore Firsts . . .

Colonel Mendes I. Cohen imported the first Egyptian antiquities collection into the United States in 1835. Eventually, the collection was bequeathed to Johns Hopkins University and put on public display in 1884.

On February 2, 1892, William Painter, an inventor from Baltimore, received U.S. Patent No. 468,226 for the idea of inserting a disc of natural or composition cork into a small piece of tin which had a corrugated rim or skirt. This was the birth of the crown cork bottle cap. Painter was the founder of the Crown Cork and Seal Company.

Joseph Heco was naturalized on June 30, 1858 in Baltimore at the United States District Court, before the Hon. William Fell Giles — thus becoming the first Japanese to be granted United States citizenship.

The refrigerator was the invention of Baltimorean Thomas Moore in 1803. Two boxes, one inside the other, separated by insulating material, made up the ancient kitchen appliance.

Homewood Field was the site of the first polo game played at night. On July 2, 1931, the Maryland Polo Club met the team from the 110th Field Artillery. Each team made use of four men.

Questions

1. The Baltimore *Sun* reported a letter that was initially sent to a newspaper in Rochester, New York. In part, it read: "I have always been more distinguished for running than fighting, and by the Harper's Ferry insurrection test, I am most miserably deficient in courage." What former resident of Baltimore wrote this letter and denied he had failed to join John Brown for reasons other than cowardice?

2. Who did *Sports Illustrated* call "THE HERO" of the 1983 World Series?

3. He came to the United States in 1981, was worth $150,000 to Baltimore, and led the Star Belgrade to three national championships. Who is this super star from Titova Uzice?

4. How many steps are there up the Washington Monument?

5. 1861 saw the nation moving steadily toward war. On April 18, the day before citizens took on the Sixth Massachusetts Regiment with rock and club, soldiers from Pennsylvania arrived by rail at the Bolton Station and marched to Camden Station to catch another train to Washington amid hissing and bricks. The Camden Station withstood the test of time. A mid-Victorian structure, the building was a reproduction of what famous American structure?

Lesser Known Facts About the Preakness . . .

It is traditionally more favorable to horses that have held the number one post position. It is also more favorable to horses that have won the Derby and later the Belmont.

Winner Polynesian (1945) sired Native Dancer (1953) who sired the 1966 winner, Kauai King.

Winner with greatest odds against him was Master Derby who won in 1975. The odds were 23 to 1.

Winner with perhaps the most questionable parentage was the one in 1961. The offspring of a horse that did not like to leave the post position — Joppy, and the less-than-showy stallion, Saggy, this horse had to overcome a 14 ¾-length lead by another horse in the first half mile. But Carry Back continued his ability to shoot from the rear of the pack and win the race. Not bad for a horse produced from a $450 mating fee.

Questions

1. Who holds the American League record for hitting into the most lifetime double plays?

2. Dr. Riccardo Giancconi was once a Fulbright scholar who, at the age of 28, abandoned pure physics for the growing field of astrophysics. In 1970 he was the major force behind the launching of the Uhuru satellite and eventually came to Baltimore to head what new project?

3. Avon Long, a graduate of Douglass High School and recognized singer and dancer, portrayed what famous character in the original Broadway production of Gershwin's "Porgy and Bess?"

4. In an attempt to close ranks among party members during the Civil War, the Republican Party used what name during their 1864 Baltimore convention when nominating Lincoln for a second term?

5. In 1903 the first American took part in the election of a Pope. Name the man who helped pick the successor to Pope Leo XIII.

The Unsolved Murder . . .

On Sunday, July 25, 1841, a beautiful young woman named Mary left her mother's house in New York City to visit her aunt. Later, aboard a ferry headed for Hoboken, Mary was seen in the company of a well dressed young man. On July 28 her naked body was found floating in the Hudson. What happened to her in partially known.

Back in New York, down at 319 Broadway, John Anderson was shaken by the death of the girl. She had worked at his cigar and snuff shop, and was probably responsible for much of its success. Her personality and beauty were said to have attracted the famous and not-so-famous; Washington Irving and James Fenimore Cooper were just two of her customers.

Newspapers competed to dig up new pieces of information on the case and rivaled each other in their coverage. Theories abounded, but no one, including the police, seemed to have all of the answers. Mary Rogers obviously had been killed.

There is no evidence to support the idea that she had fallen prey to local toughs who threw her clothes into the bushes along the river. However, there is recent and clear evidence that Mary had

(continued)

Questions

1. When the graduation class of the Colored High School held its ceremonies at Ford's Theater in 1898, it echoed the sentiments of an entire nation when it repeated the following:
   "Cuba, Cuba, bow, wow, wow! Libre, Libre, chow, chow, chow!
   Vengeance, vengeance, down with Spain! _____!"
   Complete the last line.

2. In the 1950's, a lawyer was hired to purchase a particular piece of real estate for the Duke and Duchess of Windsor in Baltimore. What did Clarence Miles acquire?

3. Baltimore is the only American League team with a winning record against what specific team?

4. During the opening game of the 1984 Orioles' season, a plane flew over Memorial Stadium with what message from a local law firm?

5. Who was the Colts coach in 1964?

The Unsolved Murder . . . (continued)

been killed by the butchering of an abortionist — not as the police thought, but as was suggested by a writer in the *Ladies' Companion*. In the short story, Mary Rogers became Marie Roget; New York became Paris; the Hudson became the Seine. Many who read it thought it a classic detective story; others who knew the author saw it as the solution to Mary's murder.

The writer, after considerable research and personal insight, proved that Mary had gone to a tavern in Hoboken owned by a Mrs. Loss. After dying at the hands of her butcher, her body was carried to the river for disposal by either the man Mary had been seen with on the ferry or Mrs. Loss' son or both of them. Who this mysterious man was has been thought to be one of a few possible figures known personally to Mary.

One man was possibly Mr. Anderson, who admitted to paying for a previous abortion. Another was the writer of the short story and a man Mary had openly dated: Edgar Allan Poe. Poe had met Mary after his arrival from Baltimore, during his early writing days in New York. It has been questioned — by modern researchers, as well as the police of the day — whether or not Poe was the father of Mary's child and the mysterious man of the ferry. He surely knew a great deal more than the police. However, the murder remains unsolved till this day.

Questions

1. Name the Hollywood actress who was born on June 9, 1926 in Baltimore as Monica Elizabeth Freeman, was hired to play in "National Velvet" as Elizabeth Taylor's sister but was considered "too mature," and made her last acting appearance on an episode of TV's "Mission Impossible."

2. In 1935, the Baltimore City Council strongly opposed United States' participation in what international event by passing a resolution?

3. Dr. William S. Halsted, chief surgeon at Johns Hopkins Hospital, is credited with the introduction of what medical items in 1894 — items that are today found in all hospitals?

4. The actual diner used in the movie "Diner" was donated to the city and can be found at what location?

5. Just prior to coming to Baltimore to be buried next to her husband, *exactly* where were Virginia Poe's remains?

Some Feel That the Local Man Never Died That Day . . .

When the news spread that John Wilkes Booth had been shot and fatally wounded following the assasination of Lincoln, the rumors seemed to begin. Every man, woman and child was interested in the strange events surrounding the death of the president of the United States and the unusual events that surrounded the death of his killer. What were some of the things that occurred, regarding the local actor from "Tudor Hall" near Bel Air?

Booth's body was returned to Washington aboard a navy flattop, and the first rumor that spread was that the man brought back from a Virginia farm was not Booth. It was thought by many — including some today — that John Wilkes Booth survived to live longer than those who hunted him.

In 1870 a man, calling himself John St. Helen, claimed to be Booth and accused President Andrew Johnson of faking the story of Booth's death and of substituting another body. In 1903 a man known as David E. George died in Enid, Oklahoma; for many years he had claimed to be St. Helen and Booth. His embalmed corpse traveled the carnival scene for decades, displayed as Booth.

One point needs to be pointed out: From the very beginning, people who could have identified the body were kept away from it. Junius Brutus Booth, Jr., John's brother, never got to see the body — even though he was being held in Old Capitol Prison (where the body was first brought) under suspicion of involvement in the crime.

Questions

1. Millard Fillmore once joined an anti-Catholic, anti-foreigner fraternal order 27 years into his political career — although he began his political life as an anti-Mason. Name this fraternal order.

2. *The Sporting Magazine* gives out its Fireman Award to the relief pitcher of the year. Who was the Oriole winner in 1963?

3. According to recorded history, the first industrial concern in Baltimore Town produced what?

4. Wilbur Hicks was a "Baltimore's Best Award" winner in February 1983. He was the all-time money winner on what TV quiz show?

5. An article in the December 13, 1908 issue of *The Sunday Sun* stated that it was first made on April 17, 1846 at 8:15 a.m. by a John Welby Henderson at the old Palo Alto Hotel in Bladensburg, Maryland for a John A. Hopkins, Esquire of Fairfax, Virginia, to settle his nerves after a successful duel. What was "it?"

This Girl Really Got Around . . .

Hetty Cary, the woman responsible for setting "Maryland! My Maryland" to music and having it performed at a meeting of a group known as The Monument Street Girls, was a member of a family who always seemed to find itself on the brink during the Civil War. In those days, the city was occupied by federal soldiers and guns were trained on downtown from Federal Hill under the direction of Union General Ben Butler.

Hetty once stood in an open window of her home and waved a Confederate flag at federal soldiers. One officer wanted to arrest her, but a colonel looked at her defiant stance and remarked: "No, she is beautiful enough to do as she damn pleases."

In April of 1865, Constance Cary, Hetty's cousin from Virginia, came to Baltimore under a flag of truce and wearing one of the oddest dresses in American history. Because Union soldiers were closing in on Richmond, many people began to flee or see to it that their valuables were spirited from the city. Constance came to Baltimore with her father's securities sewn into the lining of her gray-beige skirt. She brought them to Hetty's home and her uncle put them into a tin box and hid them. The bank that had previously held these same securities was directly hit by Union fire and destroyed the day after they had been removed by Constance.

Questions

1. What other teams did Jon Miller broadcast for prior to becoming the choice of the Orioles?

2. "Homewood" was once a wedding gift from Charles Carroll of Carrollton to his son, Charles, Jr. Part of Johns Hopkins campus today, the home was used for what purpose from 1897 to 1902?

3. When Baltimorean Thurgood Marshall graduated from Lincoln University, he actually planned to study what profession other than law?

4. During the Civil War, what special purpose was made of Baltimore Cotton Duck Extra?

5. The Glenn L. Martin Company of Middle River was the first company in the United States to make what?

The Strange Events of Mrs. Carter's Voyage . . .

Lucille Polk Stewart was one of Baltimore's reigning belles in 1899. Some years later, she became the wife of William E. Carter, a millionaire and prominent society man who owned a large estate in Bryn Mawr, Pennsylvania, and Rotherby Manor in Leicestershire, England.

At 1:55 a.m. on Monday, April 15, 1912, Lucille bade good-by to her husband and, along with her son, daughter and a governess, floated off into the dark, icy waters of the North Atlantic. William stayed behind with other trapped victims aboard the *Titanic*. Minutes later, the fate of 1,522 people was sealed, when the great ship went to the bottom. Lucille was unsure of her husband's fate.

The *Sun* of April 15 headlined: "TITANIC HITS ICEBERG, IS REPORTED SINKING." Anderson Polk, Lucille's brother, traveled to New York to get a first hand look at the situation and await word of his sister. Down at the Baltimore offices of the White Star Line, crowds that gathered were assured that all passengers had been removed from the *Titanic* and the ship was in tow to Halifax.

"On Board *S.S. Carpathia* April 17, 1912 Mrs. W. S. Polk, 2909 St. Paul St., Balt.: All Are Safe. Lucille." A wireless told of their safety. But nothing could describe Lucille's shock when she stepped aboard the rescue ship.

After the last lifeboard pulled away from the *Titanic,* William prepared to go down with the ship — just as John Jacob Astor and the other husbands of women sharing space on Boat No. 4 actually did. However, a poorly manned lifeboat floated near and Carter was asked to lend a hand. His act helped others and saved his life. Hours later, when Lucille and the children stepped aboard the *Carpathia,* there stood William who had been picked up earlier.

Pure Sports!

1. There were five horses to win the Preakness and the Triple Crown in the years prior to the United States entering World War II. Name them.

2. Name the quarterbacks for the Colts who were awarded the Jim Thorpe Trophy for MVP in pro football.

3. What player was traded by Baltimore to first obtain Frank Robinson?

4. What is the name of the parent team of the Baltimore Skipjacks?

5. Johns Hopkins is the home of the Hall of Fame for what sport? It was made the permanent home for the Hall of Fame in what year?

6. When the Blast decided Baltimore was to be its new home, two other cities were turned down. Name them.

7. On April 19, 1971 the Baltimore Bullets beat what team 93 to 91 to win the conference championship?

8. What is 34 inches tall and weighs 29 pounds 12 ounces and can be seen at the Baltimore Museum of Art when not in use?

9. What baseball team holds the record for the fewest runs scored in a World Series?

10. Name the member(s) of the Colts who made the Associated Press All-Pro Team for 1982.

90

Pure History!

1. The old United States Arsenal in Pikesville is the headquarters of the Maryland State Police. What was it used for after the Civil War?

2. In a bitter and unsuccessful convention in Charleston, South Carolina in 1860, the Democrats discovered they were going nowhere and abandoned the meeting without selecting a candidate. They reconvened in Baltimore shortly afterward and nominated what man for the presidency?

3. Name the inventor who came to Baltimore in 1876 as a trained watch repairman and whose invention was revolutionary — so inventive that its use was rejected in Baltimore.

4. What Baltimore mayor drove the bulldozer that broke ground for the creation of Charles Center in August 1966?

5. Why was Baltimore's first court house built on stilts?

6. When Abe Lincoln spoke to Baltimoreans at the YMCA on April 22, 1861, he said: "You . . . would not lay a straw in the way of those who are organizing . . . to capture this city." Of what city was he making reference?

7. Brown's Wharf in Fells Point was developed by Alexander Brown in the 1820's to handle cargo brought to port by his fleet of eleven ships. The last coffee cargo was unloaded at the wharf in 1890. Brown is most noted for the creation of Alex Brown and Sons Investment Bankers. From what country did Brown come?

8. What United States president went to school closest to Baltimore (not in the city)?

9. After becoming useless, the Battleship *Texas* was allowed to obstruct part of the Chesapeake. In 1911, she was renamed the *San Marcos* and became a target ship. In 1921 she became an important part of one man's experiments to show the powers in Washington, D.C. that battleships could be sunk by air power. Who was this man?

10. What was the impression made upon Lord Baltimore when he first saw the city in Maryland named for him?

The Finer Arts!

1. Baltimore's Ford's Theater closed the day after the final performance of what play in 1964?

2. Where would you go to find the largest collection of books in Baltimore (some 1.75 million volumes)?

3. What author penned the following plots: (a) George is the offspring of a virgin and a computer; (b) a retelling of Scheherazade; and (c) Ebenezer come to Maryland from England to take over his father's tobacco plantation?

4. "Jenny and the Phoenix" is a play that producer Joseph Papp opted for in 1977 by what local poet?

5. In 1980, Sandy Kempske of the Baltimore Zoo announced that gorillas in captivity get bored, sick and listless. A group of students at St. Paul's School for Girls made a contribution to the zoo that they hoped would spark up the spirits of the caged mammals. What did they donate?

6. Responsibility for Baltimore's Bicentennial Cake (a cake made of 10,000 eggs, 21,600 pounds of sugar, 18 tons total weight) that left an unpaid bill of $50,000 and made the *Guinness Book of World Records*, rested with what individual?

7. Name the singer-actor who had a brief stay at St. Mary's Industrial School as a youth.

8. "Beloved Infidel" was a 1959 movie that starred Gregory Peck and Deborah Kerr. What some-time Baltimore resident-personality did Peck portray?

9. What was the theme song of Cab Calloway's band?

10. In 1933 the autobiography of Gertrude Stein was published under what title?

Pure Baseball!

1. Name the player that Paul Richards decided was not batting up to par and should be sent to a farm team, *but* was stopped by protesting Oriole pitchers who told him: "We don't care if he never gets a hit. Just please leave him in there."

2. What famous player was traded by Baltimore to the Philadelphia A's in 1925 for a mere $100,000 and replaced Walter Johnson as the league's premier "smoke thrower?"

3. If he had not left the Browns in 1953 (with a 28–31 lifetime pitching record, after coming to the majors), he would have become an Oriole. Who was this hurler?

4. When chided about the fact that his $80,000 yearly salary was higher than President Hoover's, he is supposed to have observed, "Well, I had a better year." Who made this comment?

5. At the time he did it, he was the youngest pitcher, at age 20, to ever throw a shutout in the World Series. He beat the Dodgers in 1966. Name this pitcher.

6. In 1980, Steve Stone went 25 and 7, winning the Cy Young Award. Who did Earl Weaver refer to as "Cy Young," "Cy Present," "Cy Past," "Cy Future," and "Cy Future Future?"

7. Name the one-time Oriole who hit home runs in the most major league parks — at least one in 32 different stadiums during regular season games from 1956 and 1977.

8. Who created the Oriole bird for the *Morning Sun*?

9. The longest Oriole game in history took place on August 25, 1968 and took 5 hours and 20 minutes to complete. Who won the 18-inning game?

10. Name the graduate of Clemson who was signed as the Orioles' first bonus baby.

Baltimore Dates and Events

1. Henry Cavendish discovered that water was a compound of hydrogen and oxygen and John Wesley signed a deed of declaration as the charter of Methodism during this year. While in Baltimore, Maryland, Edward Warren (only 13 years old) took off over Howard's Park — now Mt. Vernon Place — in the first balloon flight in United States history. What was the year?

2. In what year did the Baltimore Harbor Tunnel open?

3. While D. H. Lawrence was publishing his novel, *Lady Chatterley's Lover* and Stephen Vincent Benét was publishing *John Brown's Body*, Baltimore's Upton Sinclair was publishing *Boston*. This was the same year that the Graf Zeppelin sailed above the city of Baltimore at the end of its first voyage across the Atlantic. What was the year?

4. In 1860, Baltimore got its first baseball team. What was the name of that team?

5. Thomas Widley and four friends started what fraternal organization (the first lodge of this group) at the Seven Stars Tavern in Baltimore in 1819?

6. In what year did world-famous Lexington Market burn down?

7. In what historic year did Mary Pickersgill, maker of the flag that flew over Fort McHenry during the British attack in 1814, come into this world?

8. On February 11 of what year did the Baltimore Symphony Orchestra perform its first public concert?

9. Elvis Presley made his last appearance in Baltimore at the Civic Center in what year?

10. In 1832 the last surviving Signer of the Declaration of Independence died in Baltimore. Name him.

Pure Football!

1. On Sunday, October 30, 1983, Raul Allegre booted five field goals in the game to tie an existing Colts record. Who did Allegre tie? Who were the Colts playing that day? Who won?

2. Johnny Unitas played for the University of Louisville. Prior to coming to Baltimore, Unitas had some semi-pro experience and was paid $6.00 per game by what team?

3. Who was with the Colts for 11 seasons, was the first pure offensive lineman to be inducted into the Hall of Fame? (Note: he was a graduate of Ohio State, started with the Colts in 1957, made All-Pro eight straight years, and made the NFL's decade team for the 1950's.)

4. Name the WMAR-TV sportscaster who blasted the Colts on live TV and was paid back the next week, when members of the team cornered him in the locker room and drenched him with Gatorade.

5. Bert Jones holds the record for the most consecutive passes completed in a single game. It was accomplished on December 15, 1974 against what team? How many passes did he complete?

6. After being behind 27–7 at half time, the Colts won their first conference title on November 30, 1958 by a score of 35–27. Who made the winning touchdown, running 75 yards?

7. Colts coach, Frank Kush, former coach of Arizona State University, was charged by one of his former players at ASU with punching him during a 1978 game against the University of Washington for making a poor punt. Name the player he supposedly hit.

8. In what year did Robert Irsay acquire the Colts? In which year of his ownership did the team have their best attendance?

9. Jim Brown scored 126 touchdowns in his NFL career. What Colt scored 113?

10. Name the coach of the 1958 victorious Colts — his real first name included.

Pure Preakness!

1. There were six horses that ran in the Preakness that had "Bold" in their names. How many can you name?

2. The first horse to wear a floral horseshoe made of "Black-eyed Susans" was the winner of the 1940 meet. Name the horse.

3. Name the member of the Maryland Jockey Club who presented the Woodlawn Vase to the 1957 Preakness winner, Bold Ruler.

4. Eddie Arcaro rode in eight consecutive Preakness runnings between 1946 and 1953. How many did he win? How many did he finish in the money?

5. Citation won the 73rd (1948) Preakness. What image was marked since birth on the head of the great thoroughbred?

6. There have been (as of 1983) only four fillies to win the Preakness. Name them.

7. The 1946 winner of the Preakness should never have made it to the starting gate — considering that it was injured by a surveyor's stake that ran into its hoof as a colt. Name the horse that was raised on the King Ranch in Texas and went on to win the Triple Crown that year.

8. The Preakness has been run on every day of the week with the exception of one. Name the day.

9. On June 16, 1945 the greatest stakes racing card ever staged on any American track was held due to wartime necessity. On that day, five major races were held — one was the Preakness. What were the other four?

10. From oldest to youngest, list the Triple Crown races.

Expert Level Baltimore Trivia

1. What is significant about "N6276J?"

2. Hypnotist, James Roday, made financially significant use of his skills to perform a rather unique service to female clients. Name the specific service he performed — one, he said that had 80 percent success and one for which no one had ever demanded their money back.

3. Who was responsible for the "Incredible Edible Eggs," the "Enfants Terrible," and "Rock Hard Peter?"

4. Name the former Baltimore sportscaster who made the *Guinness Book of World Records* for the longest kiss in 1978 — 125 hours — accomplished with the help of Candy Wessling of WKYS Radio, Washington, D.C. for the March of Dimes.

5. What was worth $268,482.00 on December 30, 1982 and was #1198 08105?

6. What was "Barnes' Brain?"

7. He and his wife were parents to the fourth "test tube" baby delivered in the world. Who?

8. While editor and publisher of the *San Francisco Examiner*, he opposed Jimmy Carter and made his own headlines, when he printed Patty Hearst's arraignment picture on its front page — the newspaper her father owned. Who was this man?

9. Name the judges that served in the first and second trials in the United States vs. Marvin Mandel.

10. What was known as "Hippie High?"

Super Expert Level Baltimore Trivia

1. Name Mayor Schaefer's barber.

2. In what year did the old Oriole ballpark in Northeast Baltimore burn down?

3. Francis Scott Key was a devout lay reader and wrote many church songs — such as "Lord With Glowing Heart I'd Praised Thee" — which is still sung in what church?

4. Name the speaker, the play and its author from which the following lines come: "We would simply like to thank the Court and the Prosecution. We agree that this is the greatest day of our lives."

5. The Maryland Jockey Club was first begun in 1743 in Annapolis. It survived a number of wars: the French and Indian, the Revolutionary, the War of 1812, and the Mexican. The Civil War ended its existence. However, following the War Between the States, the governor of Maryland saw to it that a track was established in Baltimore. As a result, Pimlico was born and the Maryland Jockey Club was reborn. Name the first postwar president of the Club — who had been the governor responsible for its revival.

6. What was razed in 1929 to make way for the Western Electric Company plant on Old Point Breeze?

7. A writer for *Time* magazine named David W. Chambers once lived in a house at 2610 St. Paul Street. What significant event hurtled him into notoriety?

8. Who, according to the Orioles, threw a "fosball?"

9. "Chamber of Horrors" was a film made in 1966 about the events that took place in what kind of a building in Baltimore?

10. Name the author of *The Last Time When* and screenwriter (along with Carl Reiner and Steve Martin) in Martin's film, "Dead Men Don't Wear Plaid."

Expert Level Baltimore History Trivia

1. The *United States Frigate Constellation* received her name, a reference to the stars in the nation's flag, from what person?

2. Four inches high, this nine-letter word was the biggest headline in the history of the *Evening Sun*. What was the word?

3. Name the first United States president to ride on a train. The trip was from Ellicott Mills (now Ellicott City) to Baltimore.

4. What life-saving procedure was jointly created by the Johns Hopkins Hospital and the Baltimore City Fire Department?

5. "Of all the women in the great Republic, Aileen is probably the most amusing." Who was H. L. Mencken speaking of when he made this statement?

6. Baltimore's first free public library was made possible by what man?

7. Name the first three streets laid out in Baltimore town.

8. Who was the first president to visit the city of Baltimore?

9. On March 29, 1878, Augustus C. Davis and J. H. C. Watts became the first men in Baltimore to create something so unique, functional and potentially lucrative that today one finds numerous successors. What was their contribution to the city's past and future?

10. Many cities around the nation can boast of having a Washington Monument — a Baltimore first. However, the city also has another statue that has the distinction of being the first to be erected to what explorer?

Very Serious Football Trivia

1. In the Colt-Cowboy contest known as Super Bowl V on January 17, 1971, held in Miami's Orange Bowl, there were a record number of turnovers (fumbles and interceptions). How many?
   AND

2. In that same game, Johnny Unitas was sidelined when he was crushed by a bruising hit by what member of the Cowboys' defensive team?
   AND

3. Who scored the winning point for Baltimore?

4. One week before playing the Cleveland Browns on November 1, 1959, Gene "Big Daddy" Lipscomb told the press that he had been "waiting a long time to get my hands on that Cleveland cat." However, when the two teams met, the "Cleveland cat" had the best day of his career — scoring five TD's — and leading his team to a 38–31 victory over the Colts. Who was the player Lipscomb wanted to get his hands on — the man that scored all but 19 of this team's 197 yards?

5. Under what coach and for what college team did Tom Matte play?

6. Name the Colt player who suffered a cracked kneecap in 1962, was slowed down by an appendectomy at the start of that season, and was sidelined for seven games in 1963 due to a head injury suffered at the end of the 1962 season.

7. He wasn't selected until the 20th round of the 1955 draft; but when he retired, he was the leading receiver in the NFL history books — with 631 receptions for 9,275 yards and 68 touchdowns. Name him.

8. What former Colt was fined $500 in 1977 for violating the NFL's dress code — because the bottom of his uniform pants did not cover the tops of his stockings (an incident that coach Ted Marchibroda called ridiculous)?

9. Name the former Colt (who retired after the 1962 season) who was bound in a chair, robbed and shot twice in a Missouri motel in January 1983 — but was able to save his wife from an attempted rape.

10. On January 23, 1953, Carroll Rosenbloom named what man as the Colts' first head coach?

100

Expert Level Mixed-Bag Baltimore Trivia

1. What was (and could still be) a "Baltimore Chop?"

2. Who composed over 2,000 pieces, including "Black, Brown and Beige" and "Solitude?"

3. Before it was discarded, upon the removal of Edgar Allan Poe's body from its first grave and placed in its second, what would you have been able to read on his headstone?

4. On June 14, 1914, 6,500 school children from Baltimore made what *and* where did they make it?

5. Sugar Ray Leonard's first professional fight was held on February 5, 1977 at 4:30 p.m. at the Baltimore Civic Center. Who was his opponent?

6. In 1839 he said: "I had rather be right than be president." Five years later this same man was sent the first telegraph message of national importance. The message informed him that he had been nominated by the Whigs to run for president. Who was the man, nominated in Baltimore and informed of his nomination 23 days before Morse is credited with sending his famous "What hath God wrought?" message?

7. World War I caused a number of things to be renamed: "liberty cabbage" had once been sauerkraut and German toast became — for all time to come — "French toast." In Baltimore, what was German Street renamed?

8. How many holes were made in the flag that flew over Fort McHenry on September 13, 1814?

9. When the Colts drafted John Elway in 1983, the Stanford quarterback remarked that he would rather play minor league baseball for a Yankee farm team than play football in Baltimore. Well, who did the Colts pick up for trading off Elway to Denver?

10. A popular game among children, skipping flat stones across water, has found players among all generations. During the early years of this nation, the game gave its name to a particular type of vessel that was built in Baltimore. Name this type of sailing ship.

Answers

Page 1:
1. Dave McNally in 1970
2. Federal Hill
3. He became an Assistant Public Defender in Baltimore.
4. Charles Street is 10½ miles in length.
5. In 1927 Walter Donaldson had a hit on his hands. With lyrics by George Whiting, "My Blue Heaven" was unusual in that it was limited in use due to the "Molly and me" at the close of the song. This close limited its use to male singers — something that pop singers, writers and publishers avoided like the plague. It should be pointed out, however, that Judy Garland didn't care about such things and recorded the song.

Page 2:
1. "Romper Room" began live in 1953.
2. Tom Matte was the substitute quarterback for injured team members Johnny Unitas and Gary Cuozzo.
3. A folded copy of his letter of resignation as commander of the army
4. *MS. Found in a Bottle* written in 1833; MS. standing for "Manuscript."
5. Blaze Starr, one-time owner of the "Two O'Clock Club"

Page 3:
1. Stein had attended Radcliffe and studied psychology under William James. She entered Johns Hopkins University and studied in the medical school, undertaking experiments in brain anatomy. In 1902 she flunked out, when her studies and academic interests were distracted by her first lesbian affair. She moved to Paris.
2. Harry and Teresa Meyerhoff owned the winning horse, Spectacular Bid, which had been ridden by Dundalk jockey Ronnie Franklin.
3. Spiro T. Agnew
4. Earle Monroe shares the honors with Joe Cadwell who played for Atlanta — 13 points. Earle scored his on February 6, 1970 against Detroit.
5. James Brown

Page 4:
1. The Basilica of the Assumption. On November 4, 1982 a commemorative walk was held from the Carroll Mansion to the Basilica in remembrance of his death 150 years before.
2. Cambridge Arms Apartments
3. McCormick and Company, of course
4. Free style discus throw
5. Sailed under San Francisco's Golden Gate Bridge

Page 5:

1. Paul Blair was with Baltimore in 1966 and 1970 and he was with the Yankees the same two years as Reggie Jackson (1977 and 1978).
2. Umbrellas
3. Longfellow's "Hiawatha" had the following lines:
   "I, the friend of man, Mondawmin,
   Come to warn you and instruct you
   How by struggle and by labor
   You shall gain what you have prayed for."
4. Francis X. Bushman
5. Between 1949 and 1973 the CIA secretly funded mind control experiments at prisons, hospitals and universities at a cost of some $25 million. Johns Hopkins University was notified that it "may" have been involved in the program, masked under various code names such as: MK-DELTA, Project Bluebird, Project Artichoke, and MK-ULTRA. At least 39 separate projects existed involving human subjects, many of whom were unaware that they were acting as guinea pigs. One such experiment involved a Dr. Frank Olson, an army biochemist at Fort Detrick, Maryland, who was given LSD as part of a 1953 experiment while working on top secret germ warfare studies. His body was later discovered at the base of the Statler Hilton Hotel in New York City — after "falling" from his 10th-floor room. His widow was awarded $750,000, after asking too many questions of the United States government.

Page 6:

1. The official substance used by umpires to rub down baseballs prior to every game
2. Next to his wife Sara in Loudon Park Cemetery
3. John Wilkes Booth, son of actor Junius Booth, was sent to Milton Academy from his home near Bel Air around 1847.
4. Barnes, an accomplished artist, was responsible for the canvas shown at the beginning and end of each episode of TV's "Good Times" produced by Lear. According to the script, the canvas was painted by J. J. Evans played by Jimmy Walker.
5. Randy "Short People" Newman on "Little Criminals"

Page 7:

1. The Beatles appeared in two performances at the Civic Center in 1964.
2. Davidge Hall at the University of Maryland (Lombard and Greene Streets) graduated its first medical class in 1813.
3. Catonsville Nine
4. "On Our Own"
5. Fort McHenry

Page 8:

1. The famous prize fighter, whose real name was James J. Corbett, had a brother, Joe, who pitched for the Orioles in the 1890's.
2. Sonja Henie
3. Mafia and La Cosa Nostra
4. Fells Point Diner
5. Bolus River

Page 9:

1. Murray was ejected on June 18, 1979 in Cleveland for arguing a call made by umpire, Fred Spenn. Spenn had called Cliff Johnson safe on an attempted pick-off at first base. Earl Weaver was also put out of the game in a later inning for arguing with head umpire, Larry Barnett, and for tearing up a rule book and throwing it on the field. Baltimore won the game.
2. "Tom Thumb" was America's first steam engine, built by Peter Cooper in 1830 at the Caton Iron Works. In a now famous race with a horse, the engine, known as the "little tea-kettle on a track," lost. This did not stop the B & O from making the transition to steam. Tom Thumb was also the name given to Charles Sherwood Stratton (also known as the "General") — a midget who appeared with P. T. Barnum periodically at Barnum's Museum in Baltimore. He stood 36 inches tall and was married in 1863 to Lavinia Warren (also known as "Lavinia Bump") — a 32-inch midget who also worked for Barnum.
3. John Dos Passos, political reporter and author
4. The great blues singer of the 1920's and the 1930's, Bessie Smith, was badly injured in a car wreck in rural Mississippi. While awaiting an ambulance, another car, driven by a drunk, ran into the wreck, causing additional injuries to Bessie. Her right arm was amputated, but shock and internal injuries caused her death a few hours later. She died on September 26, 1937 in Ward One of the Afro-American Hospital in Clarksdale. Her grave in Sharon Hill, Pennsylvania remained without a headstone until 1967, when several people, including Janis Joplin, paid for one.
5. Lenny Moore scored 20 in 1964.

Page 10:

1. President James Polk sent the message exclusively to the *Sun*.
2. Arcaro rode Whirlaway in 1941, Citation in 1948, Hill Prince in 1950, Bold in 1951, Nashua in 1955, and Bold Ruler in 1957.
3. Baltimore Manual Training
4. Fuselage Avenue was the main street of Aero Acres, a development built by the Glenn L. Martin Co. to house World War II workers employed in making the Martin Bomber. Components of the Bomber furnished names of other streets: Left and Right Wing Drive, Cockpit Street, Propeller Drive, and Dihedral Drive. By the way, its Zip Code is 21220.
5. The 1980 World Cup, one of the most prestigious equestrian events in the world, held in Baltimore in 1980.

Page 11:
1. National Bohemian Beer comes from "The Land of Pleasant Living."
2. John Cassavetes
3. The Civil War; it was dedicated in 1866
4. They were the cause of the "rockets' red glare" that Francis Scott Key mentioned in "The Star-Spangled Banner" — the British rockets fired at Fort McHenry.
5. Noxzema Skin Cream — first called "Dr. Bunting's Sunburn Remedy"

Page 12:
1. William Lloyd Garrison (1805–1879) was arrested and jailed in 1830 for what was judged an innacurate and libelous account he had written about a local merchant who was engaged in legally ferrying slaves up and down the Atlantic coast. Upon his return to Boston, Garrison began publishing *The Liberator* (first issue, January 31, 1831). The merchant was Francis Todd and he owned a ship, the *Francis*, that had sailed for New Orleans, under the direction of a captain Nicholas Brown. Garrison had charged Todd with sentencing the men to solitary confinement for life and charged Brown with domestic piracy. Benjamin Lundy published Garrison's remarks in his anti-slavery monthly. "Genius of Universal Emancipation." Garrison only went to jail because he couldn't raise the $50 fine plus costs.
2. David De Boy made the recording with his group, "The Fool Brothers."
3. Cleopatra's Needle, an obelisk
4. The movie was "Two Minute Warning" and was shot in part at Memorial Coliseum in Los Angeles. It also featured Howard Cosell and Frank Gifford as the sports announcers. Merv Griffin sang the national anthem.
5. *Moth-Eaten Mink*

Page 13:
1. Woodrow Wilson received a Ph.D. from Johns Hopkins University where his 1886 thesis was entitled, "Congressional Government, a Study in American Politics."
2. In 1980 the Orioles won 100 games and lost 62, while the Yankees won 103 and lost 59. The American League East title went to the Yankees who were beaten in the championship series for the pennant by the Kansas City Royals (who had only won 97 games all year).
3. Grace Hartigan
4. Alex Brown and Sons
5. The Palazzo Vecchio Tower in Florence, Italy. It was built in 1911.

Page 14:
1. Thurgood Marshall of the United States Supreme Court and entertainer Cab Calloway.
2. Edith Massey gave the drummer her first tryout in music.
3. On the morning of September 12, 1814, British General Robert Ross ate breakfast at the Gorsuch farm, prior to his attack on Baltimore at North Point. Legend tells us that two saddler's apprentices, David Wells and Henry McComas, shot and killed the officer. The two had been in the advance party of General John Stricker

at the city's outer defenses which were at the narrowest point of the Patapsco River when they spotted Ross. Both Wells and McComas were killed in the skirmish. Their bodies were buried in a vault in Aisquith Square; a monument was erected in 1858.

4. The 1972 winner was named Bee Bee Bee.
5. *Waverly* was the first novel written by Sir Walter Scott in 1814.

Page 15:

1. "The Defense of Fort McHenry" was published in Baltimore for the first time as a broadside and then in two newspapers — the *Baltimore Patriot* on September 20, 1814 and the *Baltimore American* on September 21.
2. The Duchess of Windsor, the former Wallis Warfield Simpson of Baltimore, once remarked that: "One can never be too rich or too thin."
3. In 1929 (November 2) a "Believe It or Not" cartoon appeared in national newspapers with the following caption: "America has no national anthem." It went on to tell how the United States, then under the laws of prohibition, was using an old English drinking song. At the same time, back in Baltimore, Mrs. Holloway waged her own campaign to make "The Star-Spangled Banner" the National Anthem. Regardless of who gets credit, the fact remains that more than 5 million letters poured into Congress as a result of the cartoon asking why something wasn't done about the situation. On March 3, 1931 Congress took action and passed a resolution making the song the nation's official anthem.
4. Moana, also known as "the sexy savage" and "the jungle queen"
5. John

Page 16:

1. These were fraternal-political organizations that were most active during the mid-1800's and took on the form of "gangs." Probably the most vicious was the "Bloody Tubs." They earned their reputation by selling election influencing services to the highest bidder. The gang's name came from their habit of dunking political opponents in slaughterhouse tubs. At one time, their turf extended to Philadelphia. Along with the "Bloody Inks," they got so out of hand between 1857 and 1870 that even the most callous politican would not use their services.
2. The judge conceded that Agnew's uncontested crime usually brought a two to five-month sentence; however, he merely fined him $10,000 and put him on probation for three years.
3. Fahlberg wiped his mouth with his hand during an experiment. The compound on his fingers tasted sweet. Together they called their new discovery saccharin.
4. St. Francis Xavier Church was founded in 1864 and built at Calvert and Pleasant Streets.
5. Bailey drove a cab.

Page 17:

1. The Baltimore Banners were joined by the Philadelphia Freedoms, the Boston Lobsters, and the New York Sets in the Atlantic Division.
2. Although she went on to become a weather girl with WBAL, Rhea Franklin's first venture was as "Betty

Betterspeech" on a show aimed at kids. She later appeared on "The Looking Glass" and "Rhea and Sunshine." A local weather spot featured "Rhea and J. P." — J. P. was a puppet.
3. Frank Robinson
4. Rudolph Valentino, the movie star, who died at 31 in 1926
5. "Grease"

Page 18:
1. The 1000-foot TV tower on TV Hill
2. Babe Ruth
3. Navy blue paper window shades that were especially popular throughout the city in years past to ward off the heat of summer days
4. Wilson Goode was elected November 8, 1983.
5. The train (Baltimore & Ohio) left Baltimore and arrived in Washington on August 24, 1835 and was observed by President Andrew Jackson.

Page 19:
1. It wasn't even close. The Court ruled 8–1 in her favor.
2. This practically forgotten play was "The Artist" and its author was H. L. Mencken.
3. Unitas passed to Eddie Hinton. The ball bounced off his fingers and into the waiting hands of Mel Renfro. The Cowboy let the ball slip away and into the hands of John Mackey who took the ball 40 yards for a TD.
4. Henrietta Szold (1860–1945)
5. Boddicker was a third baseman.

Page 20:
1. The host was motion picture and TV star Tony Randall.
2. James Rouse became the president of Moss-Rouse on West Saratoga Street by a flip of a coin. He later bought out Hunter Moss and founded the now famous James W. Rouse and Company.
3. Edgar Allan Poe died October 7, 1849 at the age of 41. He was buried in Westminster Presbyterian churchyard that year and later reburied in a new grave in the same cemetery in 1875.
4. Edgar Berman, M.D. wrote *The Compleat Chauvinist* and it was published in 1982 by Macmillan.
5. Jim Gentile hit a grand-slam home run in the first inning of a game on May 9, 1961. During the second inning, he did it again. The other player to hold the distinction was Frank Robinson who hit two in the fifth and sixth innings of a game on June 26, 1970. It should be pointed out that only one other player has accomplished this feat — Jim Northrup of the 1968 Detroit Tigers.

Page 21:
1. Frank Kush, coach of the former Baltimore Colts, used the name Mr. Owings and Jimmy Irsay, son of the owner of the team, used the name Mr. Renfield when they flew out of Baltimore during negotiations for the sale of the team in March of 1984.
2. Wife beating

3. Fifteen stars appeared on the flag. To be sure, there are a number of myths that surround the flags of the United States. One is that 13-star flags must be very old. False! The truth is that few of them were made earlier than the 19th century. Thirteen-star flags were the official national banner of the United States from 1777 until the second Flag Act of 1795, when the number of stars was changed to 15. Not until a 1912 Executive Order was anything done to control the proportions of the arrangement of stars. The flag that flew over Fort McHenry (today on display at the Smithsonian Institution) had the following arrangement:

4. Citation was the overwhelming favorite and all the other entries withdrew. The favorite had a "walkover" to collect the purse.
5. Dorothy Mays who later became engaged to J. D. Souther (who did the vocals for James Taylor) and who also did commercials for Pizza Hut, Datsun and Fava Shoes.

Page 22:
1. Raimondi's Florists have the distinction of preparing daisies with black-eyed centers because black-eyed susans do not bloom until later. About 3,000 of them are dyed by hand.
2. John Carroll, first Roman Catholic bishop in America, founded the Georgetown Academy in 1789. Behind the statue of the bishop are two very old and well-worn cannon which arrived in America aboard the *Ark* and the *Dove* in 1633.
3. The young man who made rock history with "Help, I'm a Rock" and "Brown Shoes Don't Make It" was Frank Zappa. He sang for the Mothers of Invention, giving contemporary and radical views of the times.
4. When Robert Lincoln fell onto the railway tracks, it was probably due to the fact that he had increasingly bad eye problems. When he was rescued, his hero was the actor Edwin Booth, who on this day in 1865 was on his way to visit his sister in Philadelphia. Neither had any way of knowing that Robert's father would be killed a few short weeks later by the actor's brother, John Wilkes Booth.
5. Saloons and a variety of dance halls were commonplace in Fells Point. Their popularity grew with the increased use of the harbor. Ladies of evening took over the hook of land at the west end of the Point. The second and less popular theory holds that the term hooker came from this association of the prostitutes and the "hook" of land.

Page 23:
1. Prior to moving to Baltimore in 1954, the Orioles were the St. Louis Browns. They played their last game in Sportsman's Park under management of Marty Marion. Their uniforms were brown and orange.
2. The Chesapeake and Ohio
3. "Town of the big house"
4. "An American in Paris" with Gene Kelly as the young artist and Nina Foch as the girl from Baltimore

5. The cruiser was part of Admiral Dewey's Asiatic squadron anchored in Hong Kong harbor when it received orders to join with three other ships in the attack on the Spanish fleet at the Battle of Manila on May 1, 1898. No American vessel was damaged, no one was killed on an American ship, and only eight were wounded. The entire Spanish fleet of ten ships was destroyed.

Page 24:

1. With the likes of Daniel Webster to draw crowds at the Canton Race Track, the Whigs met in Baltimore to select their party's candidate. Van Buren won on the first ballot.
2. He joined the front office of the Cleveland Browns.
3. H. R. Haldeman, President Nixon's Chief of Staff, who received an original sentence of from 2½ to 8 years and went to prison in 1977.
4. Starr claimed that she spent twenty minutes in a closet making love to John F. Kennedy in 1960. Her boyfriend, Governor Earl Long of Louisiana, was in the next room holding a party. She also said that Kennedy took the time to tell her the story of how President Harding had done the same thing in a White House closet with Nan Britton.
5. One of the most publicized examples of unpopular American historical research is Howard Chapelle and Leon Polland's challenge to the authenticity of the *Constellation*. "The *Constellation* Question" looked closely at the ship's history. In 1970 Chapelle and Polland raised the issue about the vessel that now sits in Baltimore's Inner Harbor. After being built in Baltimore (Fells Point), along with five other frigates between 1794 and 1797, it saw action against France and later Britain. She was "administratively rebuilt" in 1853 and repaired once more, prior to being finally stationed at Newport. She was moved to Boston, after becoming unserviceable. In 1953 the ship was delivered to the citizens of Baltimore to be restored. Earlier (1946) questions had been raised about the actual authenticity of the ship — especially when the Baltimore committee proposed restoration of the ship as "the oldest American naval vessel afloat." Chapelle stated that the 1853 rebuilding had so altered the vessel that what existed in 1946 was an entirely new ship — with only a percentage of the original parts being authentic. A citizen's war was waged between Chapelle and the Baltimore *Sun*, until he announced the publication of a book on the subject. Protests were leveled at the authors and an attempt was made to halt publication in 1968. Polland, an advisor and chief of construction and repair of the *Constellation* Project, rebutted Chapelle's theory. The volume was published, however, by the Smithsonian. The question of authenticity may never be resolved.

Page 25:

1. Jacob Blaustein (1892–1970) the founder of American Oil Company
2. Lot holders at Loudon Park, sympathetic to the Southern cause, offered to trade the lots they held for space in another part of the cemetery if the officials at the Park would bury Confederate dead in a selected spot. Members of families who were already interred were placed in the new section in May of 1862. These first military burials included a John Scott and another soldier named Graham. The last of these burials was in August of 1937, when Colonel Hobart Asquith (age 92) of the Maryland Cavalry was laid to rest.
3. Shoemaker rode Candy Spots to victory in 1963 and Damascus in 1967.

4. "Masquerade Party" featured panelists who tried to guess the identity of heavily-costumed guests and was hosted by Peter Donald.
5. President Warren G. Harding spoke from Fort McHenry at the dedication of the Francis Scott Key Memorial.

Page 26:
1. Sun Square
2. The song was written by Hoagy Carmichael. He also sang it in the movie.
3. This Swarthmore graduate who gave out investment advice from downtown Baltimore — advice that had national impact — was T. Rowe Price. Mr. Price died in October of 1983.
4. Sailing vessels (schooners) that have plied the waterways in and around Baltimore and the Chesapeake
5. Frederick Douglass took his name from the hero of Sir Walter Scott's *Lady of the Lake*.

Page 27:
1. Hank Bauer
2. "Elusive Butterfly"
3. Alice Roosevelt visited Baltimore on the Saturday following the fire, bringing the best wishes of her father, President Teddy Roosevelt.
4. Pimlico
5. Schmidt was a fill-in for an injured friend in an open scratch doubles bowling league. He bowled two perfect (300) games in a row at the Brunswick Crown Lanes.

Page 28:
1. In honor of the newest state — Hawaii (just after Alaska).
2. Hoggie was an uncouth youth from Mencken's boyhood — the "hero to every boy above the age of seven." Mencken credits him with designing, building and navigating the largest and fastest double-decker sled in west Baltimore.
3. Dobson appeared in the movie "Cleopatra Jones."
4. The former United States Army site, Logan Field, was located in Dundalk. It was enlarged in the 1930's and named Harbor Field.
5. Caucici worked with Maryland marble and cut the figure of Washington now seen atop the Washington Monument. The figure was actually cut from three different marble slabs.

Page 29:
1. Melissa Manchester
2. Johns Hopkins
3. He poured a soda over the head of coach Frank Kush in the team dining room.
4. It would appear that the surprise gift of a bottle of Bromo Seltzer was an innocent holiday joke. It certainly could have been used for headaches or hangovers during the up-coming Christmas holiday partying. However, what happened when Cornish took the preparation home with him was unimaginable. On December 28, his housekeeper, Mrs. Katherine Adams, came down with a terrible headache. Cornish gave her a dose of the

remedy in the blue bottle. Less than an hour later Mrs. Adams was dead of potassium cyanide poisoning. The police discovered that the cyanide had been laced throughout the popular remedy, and additional checking revealed that the same plot had been responsible for the death of another member of the Knickerbocker Athletic Club. Furthermore, it was uncovered that one Roland Molineux, a 30-year-old member of the Club, had tried unsuccessfully to have Cornish removed from his position at the Club. Molineux was the son of an army general and a rather prominent resident of New York City. Handwriting analysis of the address on the package sent to Cornish revealed that Molineux was the one who sent the poison. Important to note: Molineux owned a company that used potassium cyanide. It was more than a mere coincidence that the Club member who had mysteriously died, Henry C. Barnet, had once been engaged to a Blanche Cheeseborough — Molineux's wife. She had married Molineux shortly after Barnet's death. Well, Molineux went on trial. It was revealed that he was jealous of Cornish, due to the fact that Cornish had bested him in a weight lifting contest at the Club. When the attempt to have Cornish fired failed, the poison was prepared. However, it was Mrs. Adams who took the fatal preparation. Molineux was found guilty, after a three-week trial and sentenced to death. A reversal by the New York Court of Appeals set the man free. But fate took a hand. Instead of spending his final days in Sing Sing, Molineux ended up in an asylum and died insane in 1917.

5. *How to Play Baseball* — naturally!

Page 30:

1. "The Free Lance"
2. Electric streetcars or semi-convertibles that traveled the streets of Baltimore during the first half of the 20th century — named for the companies that built them.
3. Dominic A. Leone
4. Raymond Berry, Lenny Moore and Jim Mutton
5. The letter was written about Edgar Allan Poe, who had been found at a public polling place in a public house at 44 Lombard Street, just a few blocks from the home of Dr. Snodgrass. Although his clothing was not the same fine suit he had left Richmond wearing, a Malacca cane, that had been given to him by a friend, was still being grasped by Poe when he was found. It was suspected that he was probably not robbed. It was suspected, however, that he had been used against his will as an illegal voter in the recent Baltimore City elections. Poe was found in a bad state and taken to Washington College Hospital on Broadway where he died on Sunday, October 7 of an apparent cerebral edema caused by alcohol.

Page 31:

1. Angel Cordero, Jr. was the jockey on Codex and rode to victory in the 1980 Preakness. Some felt Codex bumped the filly, Genuine Risk, who had won the Kentucky Derby prior to coming to Pimlico (the first filly since Regret in 1915).
2. Thurgood Marshall was the successful lawyer who argued the case. In 1953 he was honored at a testimonial dinner by 500 and was described as the "conscience of America." In October of 1980 he turned down an invitation from the University of Maryland to attend the dedication of the new $4 million library for the law school named in his honor. He had been turned down for admission to the school in 1930 because he was black.

3. Jack Warden played the judge. After the world premiere of the movie in Baltimore, an after-theater party was held at the Belvedere Hotel at a cost of $25 per person.
4. "SOX SUX"
5. Edith Hamilton was Bryn Mawr's first head mistress. She was born in 1867.

Page 32:
1. James Calhoun, 1797–1803
2. Karen Needle, a 1971 graduate of Milford Mill High School
3. The Houston Summit came to Baltimore in 1980.
4. The Chesapeake and Ohio Railroad uses a cat as its logo and the phrase as its motto. The cat's name is Chessie.
5. Professional wrestling

Page 33:
1. Known as "Ukulele Ike," Edwards did the voice of Jiminy Cricket in the feature-length cartoon "Pinocchio." He made the song "When You Wish Upon a Star" famous. As for the one-time stage and screen star, he died penniless and forgotten.
2. When Reggie Jackson left Baltimore in 1977, Hammen introduced a bill that called for stiff fines for anyone who threw "anything" while attending games at Memorial Stadium. He was inspired by the fact that fans threw things at Jackson.
3. "To hell with Roosevelt, to hell with Babe Ruth, to hell with Roy Acuff!"
4. The *Minden* was an English flag of truce boat that Key had boarded. He was on the boat for 25 hours.
5. "Facedancer" signed a contract with Capital Records to record in London where they cut "About Face."

Page 34:
1. Argonaut
2. The battlefield in North Carolina was called "Eutaw Springs" and was the scene of bitter fighting on September 8, 1781 between British and American forces. Historically, both sides have taken credit for a victory. The Americans were led by two Maryland battalion commanders: Colonel John Eager Howard was one of them. The British lost 85 dead and 350 wounded, with 257 missing. The Americans lost 251 dead and 367 wounded, with 74 missing. Both sides had 692 casualties each. Today a street with the same name, Eutaw, runs through the city and part of the original tract of land.
3. The Little Tavern Shop, "Famous for Coffee and Hamburgers"
4. The Basilica of the Assumption at Cathedral and Mulberry Streets, designed by Benjamin Latrobe and dedicated in 1821
5. Booth is buried in an unmarked grave in Greenmount Cemetery. At the time of his death, Booth was identified by Dr. John F. May of Washington, who had removed a fibroid tumor from his neck the year before and recognized the scar. First, the body was locked in a storage room in Old Capital Prison in what is now Fort McNair in Washington. The key to the room was kept by Secretary of War Stanton. When the building was torn down in 1867, the bodies of all conspirators in the Lincoln assassination, plus that of Booth and Captain Wirz (the commandant of Andersonville Prison), were exhumed and reburied in a locked storeroom

in Warehouse 1 at the prison. President Andrew Johnson released Booth's body to his family, following the death of Stanton. The family picked up the body at an undertaker's establishment (Harvey and Marr) whose service door opened onto the same alley behind Ford's Theater from which Booth had fled the night he shot Lincoln. (Talk about returning to the scene of the crime!) When the body was reburied in Greenmount it still had one boot in place (the other had been cut from his injured leg and left, forgotten under Dr. Mudd's bed and later discovered by Federal soldiers). The boots had the name "J. Wilkes" stitched inside (J. Wilkes had been a name Booth had used in his early days on the stage). For those who feel, as some do, that the body in Greenmount is not that of Booth, the recovery of the boot could possibly set the record straight. However, the grave remains unmarked. Johnson had insisted that no name be incised on a headstone, due to fear that Southern sympathizers might make his birthday a memorial day.

Page 35:

1. James Ryder Randal, a young Baltimorean living in the South — teaching at a college in Louisiana, wrote, "Maryland, My Maryland" in response to a news account he had read of an incident in Baltimore. On April 19, 1861 a pro-Southern mob attacked a regiment of Massachusetts soldiers as they marched through the city to pick up a train for Washington. Carrying Confederate flags and a variety of weapons, the mob provoked the soldiers into firing: 13 civilians and 4 soldiers died. The verse was set to music by Jennie Cary who borrowed the well-known "Tannenbaum, O Tannenbaum." Local pro-Southern music publishers, Miller and Beachman, printed up the first edition, proudly using the Maryland coat of arms — but not identifying the author or arranger due to its supposedly subversive contents.
2. Dr. Kopits is the director of the Little People's Research Fund, Inc. which is dedicated to efforts to correct the orthopedic abnormalities through surgical reconstruction on dwarfs.
3. "Two For The Money" was written, directed and filmed by Bonner which he described as a light comedy adventure that is not to be taken seriously.
4. When Hunter won that game on September 7, 1975, it was a six-hit shutout (his seventh and last of that season). The final score was 2–0 the losing pitcher was Jim Palmer.
5. The United States submarine *Torsk*, a resident of Baltimore's Inner Harbor, is credited with firing the last shot of World War II — a torpedo at 2117 hours Greenwich Civil Time on August 14, 1945. At the time, it was in combat with several Japanese vessels and the final shot sank a Japanese coastal defense frigate.

Page 36:

1. Howard Head, the inventor of the "Prince" tennis racket
2. "Politian"
3. George Plimpton
4. The "Spiro T. Agnew Memorial Smoke-In"
5. In 1865 the body of the slain leader was viewed at the Rotunda of the Exchange (Gay and Water Streets). The dome, designed by Benjamin Latrobe, with the help of Maximilien Godefroy, was a popular place to promenade and view the harbor during the 19th century.

Page 37:

1. "The Ninth Inning" made in 1942 and "The Pride of the Yankees" a biography of Lou Gehrig also made in 1942
2. The *President Warfield* was the name of the flagship of the Old Bay Line that had been designed to ply the waters of the Chesapeake. During World War II she was taken over by the Navy. However, it was in 1947 that things really became exciting for the *President Warfield*. A year earlier the ship had been sold for $8,028 to the Potomac Shipwrecking Company of Washington who resold her for $40,000 to a firm calling itself the Weston Trading Company of New York. Actually, this was front for Haganah — the Palestine underground. The ship was renamed *Exodus* and scheduled to take Jewish homeseekers to Palestine. The ship carried its 4,500 passengers from the port of Sette in Southern France on July 12, 1947, arriving in Haifa on July 20. The illegal passengers were delivered, but the *Exodus* was a battered and broken ship after being assaulted by British marines. She became a symbol of the violent birth of Israel. Unfortunately, she caught fire on August 26, 1952 and was declared beyond repair. She was towed to Kishon Harbor and sold for scrap. Today you can see her steam whistle on the roof of the New York Central Iron Works in Hagerstown.
3. Key borrowed the tune, "Anacreontic Song," which was first sung at the Crown and Anchor Távern in the Strand, a popular drinking club in London (1779–1780). "The Star-Spangled Banner" is merely one of many variations of the tune.
4. Bicycle racing
5. Pellington's "Iron Horse," Unitas' "Golden Arm," Donovan's "Valley Country Club," and Brasse's "Flaming Pit"

Page 38:

1. Kenny Cooper played for 10 years with the Houston Summit. Later he became the coach of the Baltimore Blast.
2. Baltimore, during the years 1814 to 1830, was the only United States city with a silver standard. If a piece was confirmed to contain eleven-twelfths silver, it could be stamped with a miniature shield of the state.
3. Three hundred thirty-eight horses were suggested by owners and trainers for the 1981 Preakness.
4. "The Trial of the Catonsville Nine" was made in 1972 and told the story of Daniel and Philip Berrigan who were anti-war activists during the Vietnam conflict. At one point they took their rage to draft office files which they destroyed and were eventually tried for this act and convicted.
5. The mansion of Miss Mary Garret served as the museum's first repository on Mt. Vernon Place.

Page 39:

1. John Kerr
2. Haussner's Restaurant
3. The estate is known as "The Cloisters" and is operated as a children's museum.
4. Edward Bennett Williams, owner of the Orioles, on January 14, 1983 "married" the Mayor (the bride) during Earl Weaver's recognition dinner — in front of some 2,700 loyal Orioles fans.
5. During the 1966 World Series, Moe struck out 11 Dodgers in 6⅓ innings — a series record for a reliever. (After the 1970 World Series win over Cincinnati, Moe gave Bowie Kuhn a hotfoot in the locker room.)

114

Page 40:

1. Henry Clay refused to make the make an acceptance speech before the nominating convention of Whigs that met in Baltimore in May of 1844.
2. She was the first American-born singer to make a debut at the Met with no previous training or experience in a foreign country. Her first role at the Met (at age 21) was as Leonora in "La Forza del Destino." She played opposite Caruso.
3. Jimmy Dykes
4. The movie about Cuban rightists who are spying for the United States starred John Forsythe and Roscoe Lee Brown. It was "Topaz."
5. Charles I, King of England was tried by such people as Oliver Cromwell and sentenced to death. He was beheaded in January of 1649.

Page 41:

1. On November 11, 1918 at 11:01 a.m., Private Henry Gunther of Baltimore died. In his official order of the day, General John Pershing announced the death of the member of Company A, 313th Infantry, 79th Regiment who was shot in the left temple and side during an ambush near Metz. It is ironic that at the moment a German bullet took Gunther's life, a messenger was arriving with the announcement that the armistice had taken place ending World War I. He made history becoming the last American to die in the war.
2. *The New Yorker* magazine
3. The *Constellation* was launched on September 7, 1797. Six weeks later the *Constitution* was launched. "Old Ironsides" is younger.
4. In 1964 the Colts won 12 games, lost 2, and became the NFL Western Conference champs.
5. "I Wonder Park" was a half-acre park created across the street from John William's tavern on Clinton Street in 1901. It was a popular relaxation spot with dock workers until it was destroyed by the Maritime Commission to build an office/warehouse in 1941.

Page 42:

1. The phrase "Triple Crown" was originated by Charles Hatton, columnist for the *Daily Racing Form*, in the 1930's. He borrowed the phrase from a long-used concept called the English Triple Crown that dated back to the early 19th century. The first Triple Crown winner was Sir Barton in 1919.
2. Following the 1904 fire, the mayor and the Board of Police Commissioners reported that "Not a single case of plundering happened, no serious depredations or losses were reported, or a life lost, though danger seemed present at every turn for days." Not one case of looting was reported by the authorities. To insure that looting did not become a problem, nearly 2,000 soldiers were placed on duty from February 8 through the 23rd. City Council had to face a number of needs in the burned out area and a major reconstruction. The Citizen's Emergency Committee met daily; the mayor and four citizens constituted the Burnt District Commission. They had powers to initiate legislation for suggested improvements and carry out the work within the fire line. Shortly after its formation the mayor declared the Commission to be virtually useless. While all this was going on, tragic events occurred. On May 30, Mayor McLane, who had been married only sixteen days, committed suicide by putting a bullet through his right temple.

3. Charles Carroll of Carrollton turned the first shovel of earth to initiate construction of the B & O Railroad. In the end the railroad won the competition for transportation supremacy.
4. Howard Schnellenberger
5. Fort McHenry

Page 43:

1. In 1902, at the age of seven, George Herman Ruth was sent to the St. Mary's Industrial School in Baltimore because his parents felt he had the potential of becoming a juvenile delinquent. He was at the school from 1902 until 1914, and during this time was befriended by a six-foot six-inch Xaverian brother named Mathias. He helped Ruth develop his baseball talents. In the 1948 movie, "The Babe Ruth Story," his role was played by Charles Bickford.
2. Male Central High School
3. Karl Sweetan of the Detroit Lions connected with Pat Studstill in a 1966 game against the Colts and pulled off a 99-yard TD.
4. The first recorded clock made in America was produced by black inventor and genius Benjamin Banneker in 1754.
5. UCLA

Page 44:

1. Uncles became the first black American Catholic to be ordained as a priest. The Baltimore-born man was baptised in 1875 at St. Francis Xavier Church and confirmed in 1878. He was ordained in 1891.
2. On February 17, 1817 Baltimore installed gaslights on a street and became the first city in the world to have such street illumination. That same month witnessed the organization of the Gas Light Company. Less than a year earlier, Rembrandt Peale demonstrated the practical use of gas lighting for buildings at his museum to startled onlookers.
3. Her name would appear under the heading: "Cheerleaders." This local girl lost her position with the Colt cheerleading squad after posing for *Playboy* magazine in the March 1979 issue.
4. Fort McHenry
5. Barbara Mikulski of the United States House of Representatives for the Third District

Page 45:

1. Two Baltimore brothers decided that there was money to be made from the popular fad of the day — spiritualism. As toymakers, they came up with an idea that really took off and became one of the most famous American products ever conceived. What was the toy? The Ouija board! The Fuld brothers were interested in an item that would be popular with the masses and give people a taste of tricks used by professional spiritualists. They simply came up with a flat board that was imprinted with the letters of the alphabet and the numbers one through ten. They included three words: "yes," "no," and "good-bye." To give the impression that spirits were talking to the players or sending them messages, the Fulds came up with a small, three-legged or three-cornered or heart-shaped device (a planchette) made of wood that served as the pointing instrument that moved by "involuntary muscular action" across the board and spelled out the

messages or answers to questions. The popularity of the Ouija board was something that even Issac and William Fuld could not predict. Patented in 1892, millions were sold — especially during World War I, among families and friends of soldiers serving in Europe. During World War II the same phenomenon occurred. But during the 1920's the rage cooled, with a minimal and constant number of sales continuing to come in. In 1966 Parker Brothers purchased the rights to the world-famous game. One of the most bizarre incidents that is related to the Ouija board occurred in the early 1930's. One Mattie Turley claimed that she was sent a message through the board to kill her father so that her mother could be free to marry her lover. She carried out the board's instructions.

2. The candidate was James K. Polk; the party was the Democratic. Here is the story: The party met in Baltimore on May 27–29, 1844. President John Tyler had withdrawn from competition early — he had been abandoned by the major parties. Polk did not even receive a single vote until he was suggested as a compromise candidate after the eighth ballot revealed that a stalemate existed between former President Van Buren and Lewis Cass. Polk was nominated on the ninth ballot. Some interesting things occurred following the nomination: (1) Silas Wright, Polk's vice presidential nominee declined his selection — the first time a convention nominee refused; George M. Dallas was selected as his replacement; (2) during the campaign that followed, various smear tactics were employed. One such tactic accused Polk of branding his initials on the shoulders of 43 slaves he supposedly owned; and (3) although Polk won the election, he lost his own state.

3. *End of the Road*

4. The quote comes from Bert Jones, former Colt quarterback, who said this when asked by an Atlanta sports writer if he still argued with owner Robert Irsay.

5. "Bosom Buddies"

Page 46:

1. Metros

2. "Hot l Baltimore"

3. "Babe Ruth's Home Run Candy" was stopped by the Curtiss Candy Corporation on a patent violation.

4. Poe's head, a raven, and his epitaph: "Quoth the Raven, 'Nevermore' " are found on the monument located at Westminster Cemetery (once called the Presbyterian Cemetery) at Fayette and Greene Streets. The large monument, just inside the gates of the burial ground, is mysteriously visited each year by an unidentified female who leaves behind roses and brandy.

5. Bromo Seltzer

Page 47:

1. Matthew Henson walked all the way from his native home in Washington to take up a brief residence in Baltimore. There he signed up as a cabin boy and sailed aboard the *Katie Hines* for five years. In 1887 he became the valet to a young navy lieutenant named Robert E. Peary on his assignment to Central America. Henson was Peary's assistant in 1886 when Peary made his first Arctic expedition. Peary was difficult to live with and Henson suffered as a result of Peary's personality and prejudices. Peary called Henson "my colored boy" and "a dark-skinned, kinky-haired child of the Equator." He even went so far as to state that he doubted a Negro could survive the climate of the North. The problems only increased when Peary took

full credit for reaching the North Pole on April 6, 1909 when, in fact, Henson was the one who got there first. The truth of the matter was a long time in coming and required the efforts of Herbert M. Frisby of Baltimore. Frisby, a graduate of Howard University, Columbia and NYU, researched the true events of the expedition and fought to get Henson the recognition he deserved. As result of his efforts, Matthew Henson was selected as a member of the famous Explorer's Club in 1937. It may not have seemed important to Robert Peary, but Henson reached the Pole 45 minutes before the admiral. Henson died in 1955.

2. McCulloch v. Maryland (1819) was a case that resulted in a historic United States Supreme Court decision that is studied by every student of constitutional law. James McCulloch was a Baltimore banker who, in the early 19th century loaned to himself some $500,000 and later refused to pay $15,000 in Maryland taxes on the bank. In a unanimous decision read by Chief Justice John Marshall, the Court upheld the federal right of incorporation (the Second Bank of the United States) and denied states (Maryland) the right to interfere in taxation. The case is important because it gave high judicial sanction to the implied powers of Congress.

3. Upton Sinclair, the muckraker, is largely overlooked by today's readers. But his 1906 novel, *The Jungle*, was a sensation in its attack on the unbelieveably unsanitary conditions that existed in the American meat industry — and a tremendous influence on the federal government.

4. Al Bumbry

5. The winner of the 1903 Preakness was Flocarline; in 1906 it was Whimsical who crossed the finish first; Rhine Maiden won in 1925; and Nellie Morse won in 1924. In 1906 the second-place horse was Content; and in 1980 Genuine Risk "placed."

Page 48:

1. Lincoln suspended the writ of habeas corpus on April 27, 1861 in an area reaching from Philadelphia, Pennsylvania to Washington. He did so, in part, to slow down and hopefully halt the turmoil in Baltimore. Enforcement of this decision was left up to General Winfield Scott.

2. This frequent visitor to Baltimore was F. Scott Fitzgerald, who met Zelda Sayre while serving in the army in Alabama. They married following the success of *This Side of Paradise*. She spent time in the facilities of Sheppard-Pratt, thus giving her husband time to produce some short stories. His first really successful work was *Tales of Jazz Age* in 1922, first printed in the *Saturday Evening Post*.

3. Ray Murray, "The Deacon," was a catcher for the 1954 Orioles. He holds the distinction of being the only catcher to ever be thrown out of a game for praying. He was ejected by umpire Ed Hurley during a game against the White Sox. Murray knelt over home plate, stretched his arms toward heaven, and prayed for better calls from the umpire. Jimmy Dykes, Orioles manager, was also tossed out when he protested the decision. Murray later said he actually prayed: "Oh, Lord, where does the pitch have to come to be a strike. This s.o.b. — same ol' boy — is still blind." The Orioles lost the game 4-3.

4. Liberty ship, of which 384 were built — each being 441 feet, 7½ inches long, by 56 feet, 10¾ inches wide and able to carry 10,500 tons of cargo.

5. The first published pieces of composer and musician Eubie Blake

Page 49:

1. On that fateful day, Gene "Big Daddy" Lipscomb arrived a few seconds after Marchetti had made a crucial tackle on Frank Gifford. The resulting injury cost Marchetti his position on the post season Pro Bowl team. The tackle did stop a Giant drive and the Colts won the game.

2. Dr. R. Adams Cowley
3. Victor Frenkil, well known contractor and owner of the Belvedere Hotel, is widely appreciated for his ability to fold paper money into two- and three-letter monograms. Some estimates given state that he has given away about $40,000 in $1 bills. He has given monograms to every United States president since Harry Truman. Frenkil asks that a reciprocal dollar be sent to the American Cancer Society.
4. The Capitol dome in Washington, D.C.
5. A case of imported champagne

Page 50:

1. Dr. Taussig specialized in rheumatic fever and heart malformation and formulated the theory for corrective surgery on what are known as "blue babies." Her colleague, Dr. Alfred Blalock performed the first successful surgical procedure in 1944. Prior to this, it was tested on a dog. The heart operation is called the Taussig-Blalock heart operation.
2. Since no known locomotive could have negotiated this curve, a solution did not quickly appear. However, New York transplant Peter Cooper jumped to the rescue and built the solution — Tom Thumb, the miniature steam locomotive. On its initial run the engine proved itself capable of handling the curve. While returning from that run, with a coach full of company executives and other VIP's, Tom Thumb was met by a horse-drawn rail car and a challenge was issued. Eager spectators awaited the match race, and most of them wanted to see the new example of the Industrial Revolution beaten. Cooper took the challenge in stride, and the race began. Initially, the horse-drawn coach took the lead but the little engine overtook its competitor. Just as the horse's driver was about to call it quits, the blower belt on Tom Thumb slipped from its drum. This spelled the end for Mr. Cooper's invention and a victory for his opposition. But talk about hollow victories: the B & O decided to invest in the boiler on wheels and, in turn, the pioneer of all railroads was saved from financial destruction.
3. Billy Martin
4. The Baltimore Ravens are a wheelchair basketball team.
5. On July 8, 1889, Jake Kilrain participated in a dying "art." He was not alone. John L. Sullivan, the American heavyweight champion, joined him. Together, the two of them would fight the last championship bareknuckle fight on record. On that day in Richburg, Mississippi, Sullivan and Kilrain, unlike modern boxers, were to fight it out until one of them did not get back up from the canvas. Rounds in those days were not merely three minutes long, but were as long as was needed to deck your opponent. This meant that the fight might take hours to resolve. The day of this historic event, the temperature had risen to 107 degrees in the heat of the summer afternoon. Sullivan had been complaining of stomach cramps — possibly brought on by the sun in conjunction with his diet (which had consisted of a breakfast that included five eggs, a whole sea bass, a half-loaf of bread, six tomatoes, and a single cup of tea). Sullivan's manager refused his request for a drink of whiskey to quell the discomfort. However, on the other side of the ring, Kilrain was doing just the opposite — swilling bourbon before the fight and between rounds. Well, what was the result of this brawl? The Baltimore boy got beat. It took 75 rounds, but the boy got beat. Sullivan went on to defend his title — wearing gloves and fighting James J. "Gentleman Jim" Corbett. Jake Kilrain returned to Baltimore to live out his life as a local bartender and celebrity — dying in 1937.

Page 51:

1. The wealthy and flamboyant "Diamond Jim" Brady who was very pleased with the success of prostate surgery he had performed at Johns Hopkins
2. The Monument Street landfill
3. Native Dancer
4. Brown's capture at Harper's Ferry was made possible by the crushing raid on his 22-man group of raiders by a contingent of United States marines under the command of Lieutenant Colonel Robert E. Lee, who had been called from his home in Arlington, Virginia.
5. The Washington Monument. Mills was responsible for designing the first monument of its type in the country here in Baltimore. Later, he designed the 220-foot obelisk at Bunker Hill in Boston. His mightiest monument is the huge obelisk in Washington, D.C.

Page 52:

1. "Maryland, My Maryland"
2. In 1969 the New York Jets beat Baltimore 16-7. In 1971 the Colts beat the Dallas Cowboys 16-13. 16 is the winning score in both games.
3. 51-year-old Democratic Representative, George H. Fallon
4. Murphy was a Barnum giant, weighing in at 351 pounds and standing 8-feet tall. He died in Baltimore in 1875.
5. Catherine Devine made history when she danced at the Chicago World's Fair in 1893 as "Little Egypt." Kernan booked her into Baltimore, following her shocking performance of her "muscle dance." The police closed down the show at "The Monumental."

Page 53:

1. Bert Jones
2. The man on the tape was Reg Murphy the editor for the Atlanta *Constitution*. He was kidnapped and, as a UPI report headlined: "Rightist kidnapers demand $700,000 ranson for Murphy." The newspaper was expected to buy his freedom and the Atlanta Newspapers, Inc., part of the Cox newspaper group, was willing to do just that. Murphy was freed on February 2, 1974. His kidnappers, Betty Ruth and William Halm Williams were captured. The money was recovered. Today Reg Murphy is the president and publisher of The A. S. Abell Publishing Company, publishers of the *Sun* papers.
3. The campus of Johns Hopkins University
4. "Kitty Foyle"
5. Jimmy Carter

Page 54:

1. Ken Singleton and Eddie Murray
2. Gamal Abd-Al Nasser of Egypt
3. The Gun Club of Baltimore

4. The "Edgar" — the Oscar of the detective novel is awarded each year. Ellery Queen received more awards than any other writer of criminal fiction, including five Edgars.
5. "I've Got a Secret," "Three on a Match" — which he took over from Bill Cullen, and "To Tell the Truth" — which he took over for Bud Collyer

Page 55:

1. Johnny Unitas
2. Scrod, according to the stories, was the name given to the first catch that fishing boats would haul in each day. This catch was subsequently smothered by the rest of the fish caught during the day. Returning to port, the first catch of the day was the last removed from the boat and sold at a discount.
3. Francis Scott Key
4. George Herman Ruth got his nickname in 1914 — according to legend — from Jack Dunne, owner-manager of the Baltimore Orioles of the International League. Dunne signed the 19-year-old that year and Ruth became his "new babe."
5. Swampy Harbor Field

Page 56:

1. The name of his play was *Home of the Brave* — the lines were borrowed from "The Star-Spangled Banner."
2. Jacks
3. The British had pulled out of Washington, after some 24 hours of plundering, and headed for Baltimore — which offered a more profitable plunder.
4. An American portrait painter, with very limited knowledge of electricity, was able to obtain the information he needed to pull off one of the greatest inventive acts of all time. Samuel F. B. Morse studied art in England under the direction of Washington Allston and returned to the United States where he became quite recognized for his talent. In 1829 he lost his wife and took an extended vacation to Europe to lose himself in her art galleries. But on his way home aboard the packet *Scully*, Morse heard a lecture on the subject of electricity and his interest was sparked. In 1836, after being soundly trounced in a run for office of New York mayor, Morse began to concentrate on the invention that would make him famous — the telegraph. In 1844 a practical demonstration led to Congressional support for the establishment of the first long-distance telegraph line from Washington, D.C. to Baltimore. $30,000 was approved by Congress and the lines (rope made of yarn and covered with tar) were set up. On May 24, 1844 Annie Ellsworth, daughter of a friend of Morse, sent what historians commonly recognize as the first message over the telegraph: "What hath God wrought?" The message was received at the Mount Clare Station by Morse's Assistant, Alfred Vail. The truth of the story is, however, that it was Joseph Henry who actually invented the telegraph for which Morse took full credit and fame. Henry was a noted American physicist with whom Morse had dealt and from whom he gathered his information. Morse denied any involvement with Henry, and so the physicist took Morse to court — where Henry proved his case. Morse was, however, an excellent promoter, and it was through these efforts that he was able to get the money from Congress to establish the line from Washington to Baltimore. Morse should be given credit for the Morse code — which he did create. He became very wealthy from the telegraph — not from painting.
5. Tripleheader

Page 57:

1. Agnew was a member of the Baltimore County Board of Zoning Appeals.
2. The Colts hold the record for the most penalties in a single season. In 1979 they amassed 137.
3. Fort Carroll was built under the direction of Robert E. Lee (then a Colonel).
4. Ron Hansen, a shortstop, was the Orioles' first Rookie of the Year in 1960.
5. Benito Mussolini — by singing arias to him in Italian

Page 58:

1. Clarence Mitchell, Jr.
2. Eubie Blake
3. Dr. Oliver Wendell Holmes
4. Gertrude Stein (1874–1946) left Baltimore in 1902 and went to Europe. After her death, her art collection was worth some $16 million.
5. The means the *Sun* was announcing was the Overland Pony Express, which had been exclusively established for the paper — with no other newspaper in the country having the service. What the readers were led to believe was that the news was brought all the way to Baltimore by an unbroken chain of horsemen from New Orleans. It was not the case; the *Sun* employed riders only in areas that were not covered by rail or telegraphic communications.

Page 59:

1. John Henry "Doc" Holliday was a practicing dentist who also killed a few men and was a personal friend of Wyatt Earp.
2. Roy Campanella
3. The advertising salesman for the Baltimore *News American* was the first victim of the "Denver Boot" (used by Transit and Traffic).
4. Four died and 24 were wounded.
5. Woodrow Wilson won the Nobel Prize for Peace

Page 60:

1. Martin Van Buren
2. "Mama" Cass Elliot died in 1974. Even the news reports told that her doctor felt she died while eating a sandwich. An official coroner's report denied the ham sandwich story. It concluded that she died of a heart attack brought on by obesity — she weighed 220 pounds (twice the weight for a woman her height).
3. In 1982 Ripken hit the grand-slam against the Yankees.
4. Nick Charles
5. She served as a communications center and was an Atlantic Fleet flagship.

Page 61:

1. The man was President Franklin Pierce who ran down a Mrs. Lewis on the streets of Washington in 1853.
2. Moe: Rick Dempsey; Larry: Rich Dauer; Curly: Todd Cruz — the Three Stooges of the Baltimore Orioles

3. Judd Hirsch of TV's "Taxi" and the motion picture "Ordinary People"
4. Cole's Harbor
5. Fort McHenry served as a POW camp to hold Confederate prisoners and sympathizers. Twenty-nine prisoners died there and were later buried at Loudon Park Cemetery.

Page 62:

1. George Blanda who had one season as a Colt
2. Paper coins, also known as Baltimore City Certificates, were issued as a result of the financial instability and threat of panics that swept the city early in the 19th century (there was a panic in 1837). Considering that there was a lack of small change, the city created its own paper coinage in a variety of denominations, such as 6¼ cents. These certificates were authorized by the mayor and city council.
3. The Belvedere Hotel
4. Young Poe refused to attend drill formations and classes for several weeks; and when he finally showed up for inspection, he did so stark naked. He was kicked out of West Point.
5. Charles Center

Page 63:

1. Betsy Patterson was a most popular young and very eligible woman. Betsy was the niece of Sam Smith (local hero of many battles) who urged her to pursue a handsome Frenchman named Jerome, who was a member of the Diplomatic mission in Washington. It was said that at one ball given by Thomas Jefferson, people could not take their eyes off of her classic features. However, Jerome won her heart and hand in marriage. Jerome, only 19, married Betsy, then 18, on Christmas Eve in 1803. The ceremony was performed by Bishop John Carroll. This did not please Jerome's brother — Napoleon Bonaparte. He did all in his power to have Jerome leave his new bride, and eventually the scheme worked. Napoleon was not impressed by Sam Smith's plan to keep the marriage together: Smith had thought that if the Catholic archbishop of Baltimore married the two, a papal annulment would be impossible. Napoleon needed sisters-in-law of royal blood — not an American. Jerome was enticed to leave his wife and their son, Jerome Napoleon, for a royal position of his own. Jerome left the United States, married Princess Catherine of Wastemburg and became the King of Westphalia. By the way, Pope Pius VII never did annul the marriage to Betsy and Madame Bonaparte was pensioned eventually by the French government.
2. The rumor, although false, held that Frank Zappa was the son of "Mr. Greenjeans" — probably because of the song, "Son of Mr. Green Genes," that appeared on an album produced by Zappa, titled "Hot Rats."
3. Ron Shapiro
4. Jimmy Orr was knocked unconscious on November 21, 1965 in a game against the Eagles. He was taken to Union Memorial Hospital, checked out, released, and rushed back to the game by ambulance. He caught a Unitas pass to win the game. Don Shula was the coach.
5. The name of the colt was Preakness.

Page 64:

1. Henri Matisse was heavily supported by the Cone sisters of Baltimore.
2. *The City Squeeze*

3. Witchita Wings; the Blast won
4. He married Carmela, sister of Rosa Ponselle. Like her sister, she also sang with the Metropolitan Opera Company — as a soprano.
5. Chris Hinton wore no Colt emblems on his all white helmet.

Page 65:
1. Emily Post
2. Jim Murray wrote a rather negative article on the 1983 World Series for the *Los Angeles Times*. "Baltimore," he wrote, "is a town with a massive inferiority complex. With much to feel inferior about." Fortunately the vast majority of Baltimoreans do not agree with Murray's feelings.
3. Black Aggie is the nickname of a copy of "Grief" by Augustus Saint-Gaudens which sat in Druid Ridge Cemetery — marking the grave of General Felix Agnus. Today she is owned by the Smithsonian in Washington. The bronze angel sat shrouded upon the grave of the Civil War soldier and newspaper man until 1967 when the cemetery officials felt she attracted too much attention from Halloween spectators and pranksters.
4. The horse was co-owned by President Jimmy Carter.
5. The flag (Star-Spangled Banner) was hidden in the depths of the Luray Caverns during World War II to protect it from any possible bombing attacks.

Page 66:
1. The Baltimore Oriole was so named because its colors — orange and black — were the family colors of Lord Baltimore, original founder of the Maryland colony.
2. Walter Mondale, Jesse Jackson, and Gary Hart — all Democrats
3. One hundred twenty-six pounds
4. The family owned the first American yacht.
5. On December 27, 1784 Francis Asbury was made the nation's first Methodist Episcopal bishop. It was at the Lovely Lane meeting house that the Methodist Church was begun in the United States. Asbury was known to cover some 270,000 miles on the American frontier between 1771 and 1816. He preached to settlers in the West in any place he could find to set up: camp meetings, riverboats, bordello parlors, and even churches.

Page 67:
1. James Buchanan
2. "The Lady Came From Baltimore"
3. Baseball signals seem to be traceable to the 1870's and they became accepted in 1894. Two Orioles, John McGraw and Wee Willie Keeler, are credited with coming up with signals for hit-and-run plays.
4. On August 6, 1914 the First Lady died. She was Ellen Axson Wilson, wife of President Woodrow Wilson — the man nominated by the Democrats in Baltimore in July of 1912. She had died from complications of tuberculosis of the kidneys, but rumors had started that her husband had arranged her death. Following his wife's death, the President went into a deep depression that lasted several months — however, the public lost its sympathy very quickly. Just 16 months after Ellen died, Woodrow met, courted and married Edith Bolling Galt. The gossip began. One rumor stated that Wilson had met and fallen in love with Edith while

his first wife was still living. Another held that he had conspired with his wife's doctor to kill her with poison. Then there was the one about Ellen finding out about Woodrow's plans for a divorce and confronting him about his affair; in this rumor, Woodrow pushed her down the White House stairs, killing her. And since he was the president, everything was carefully covered up. Time healed the situation and the second Mrs. Wilson and the President did have some peace. When Wilson suffered a disabling stroke during his last term, the second Mrs. Wilson actually took over the reins of office, making some decisions and keeping important people from him. He left office alive but feeble. Edith was often referred to as the first woman president of the United States.

5. Anyone who voted for Herbert Hoover

Page 68:

1. The Whigs met and nominated the Know-Nothing ticket of Millard Fillmore and Andrew Jackson Donelson. The Know-Nothing Party emulated the Masons in its secrecy; it was formed on pro-American, anti-foreign and strongly anti-Catholic beliefs. The name for the group came from that the fact that when members were questioned about their activities, they were instructed to say that they "knew nothing." A following developed in the early 1850's and by 1854 the group had electoral success — especially in the South. However, life was short for the Know-Nothings and it became more and more dangerous to be a member. Today the term is heard, although infrequently, to describe groups far to the right or reactionary.
2. The MGM movie, "Diner"
3. David Zinman was with the Rochester Philharmonic.
4. The *Baltimore Business Journal*
5. "The Devil Is a Woman"

Page 69:

1. Jim Gentile
2. Leon Uris was the former newspaper boy who went to war and wrote *Battle Cry*.
3. Edward Bennett Williams, owner of the Orioles
4. Glenn Doughty was sacked by Mike McCormack.
5. He perfected the technique of preserving vegetables and fruit in cans.

Page 70:

1. Strawberry Alarm Clock
2. Goddard organized the first postal system in Baltimore to rival the existing British one.
3. It did no good for DeCinces. He did not hit in four attempts at the plate. And on top of that, he made an error. What he did was to shave off his moustache.
4. Wrong, if you said F. Scott Fitzgerald. It was Gertrude Stein who overheard a French garage owner refer to his young mechanics as "un generation pedue."
5. Jane Fonda and her husband, Tom Hayden

Page 71:

1. Al Kaline is a member of the Hall of Fame and went into TV broadcasting of Tigers' games.
2. The Bachelor's Cotillion — the German and the Cotillion are intricate marches or "figures" that open a debutant ball.
3. The stirrups and bit form the letter "M" and a jockey's whip forms the letter "J." The "C" is actually the shape of a spur.
4. Private Drew was arrested for sleeping on guard duty on November 14, 1880. It is thought that during a cleanup detail prior to being locked up, Drew was able to slip a rifle into his cell in the guardhouse. He later used the rifle to commit suicide.
5. Flapper

Page 72:

1. Dillon Grey
2. Charles Carroll's Mount Clare
3. On October 16, 1983, they drank Great Western Champagne.
4. The man was Alger Hiss. He was charged with espionage and subversion by Whittaker Chambers, an ex-Communist courier. Chambers told a 1948 House hearing committee that Hiss, a former State Department official and then head of the Carnegie Endowment for International Peace, had been a member of the Communist Party for years. Hiss sued his accuser for libel. President Truman dismissed the 1948 affair as a so-called "red herring" that had been arranged by the committee to take heat off the many failures of the 80th Congress. When Chambers produced microfilm hidden in a pumpkin in a pumpkin patch, the committee felt that it had hard evidence that the classified State Department documents had been passed on to a spy ring — one that Hiss belonged to. After a second trial in 1949, Hiss was sentenced to five years. The affair was just the beginning of a period of American history known today as the McCarthy Era.
5. Barnum's City Hotel could be found on the southwest side of North Calvert Street at Fayette. It was built in 1826 and torn down in 1889. Its owner, David Barnum, died in 1844 — 17 years before John Wilkes Booth supposedly hatched his plot to kidnap Abraham Lincoln and planned it with Samuel Arnold — possibly in the hotel's barber shop.

Page 73:

1. These are a few examples of what members of the 1958 Colts did after retiring from active pro football. George Shaw (Quarterback) was the Portland stock broker and vice president of his own firm; a cornerback, Johnny Sample, bought his own sporting goods store in Philadelphia; Fred Thurston, known as "Fuzzy" to fans, operated a steak house in Wisconsin; and Don Shinnick, a linebacker, was an insurance agent in Missouri.
2. The Palm Room
3. Carroll was making reference to the opening of the B & O Railroad.
4. Bozo the Clown — the original
5. Milton Eisenhower was the running mate — even though Anderson knew that the name could be dropped after the primaries. Eisenhower remarked: "At the age of 80, I'm not a candidate for anything." Another running mate was independent Robert Flanagan — an attorney at Weinberg and Green.

Page 74:
1. The script was written by a native of Baltimore, Barry Levinson, of "Diner" fame, and his wife, Valerie Curtin.
2. The Touchdowners
3. Secretariat
4. Damon Evans
5. In 1832 (May 21–23), the first Democratic convention was held. A rule was established requiring a two-thirds majority for nominations of candidates to be valid. Representatives from 23 states met in Baltimore and on the first ballot nominated Andrew Jackson for president and Martin Van Buren for vice president.

Page 75:
1. Dwight Schultz (first name William) portrayed Murdock on TV's "The A-Team," which was labeled the bloodiest show on TV. This is the show that paired George Peppard with Mr. T.
2. Chick Webb who grew up at 1313 Ashland Avenue, who was a contemporary of Duke Ellington, and who suffered from TB and died from its effects at Johns Hopkins Hospital in 1939.
3. Damscus won and Spiro Agnew, then governor, presented the Woodlawn Vase.
4. Congressman Long was a former professor of economics at Johns Hopkins University.
5. Elizabeth Ann Bayley was born in New York and later came to Baltimore (1807) as Elizabeth Ann Bayley Seton. It was here that she started a school for girls. Two years later she took her vows and later became "Mother" Seton. She was the founder of the Daughters of Charity. Pope Paul VI made her a saint on September 14, 1974. Thus she became America's first saint.

Page 76:
1. The batter was Cleon Jones of the Mets. He was hit by a pitched ball and was given first base after an argument. The next batter was Donn Clendenon and he hit his third home run of the Series. The Mets won the game 5–3. They won the Series in five games (4–1).
2. Walcott was killed at the Little Big Horn, along with General Custer and other members of the 7th Cavalry. His body is buried at the military cemetery established at the National Park in Montana.
3. McLane was our French Ambassador in the 1880's.
4. The Edgar Allan Poe Award
5. Walter Orlinsky

Page 77:
1. Ross Grimsley
2. Blaze Starr
3. "Shuffle Along" by Eubie Blake, who hired dancer Josephine Baker
4. Frederick Douglass
5. H. L. Mencken

Page 78:
1. Tydings was the subject of a hoax. The public had a tremendous fear of anything that smacked of Communism. And numerous unscrupulous politicians used this fear to their own benefit: Joe McCarthy, Richard Nixon, and John Marshall Butler. Butler had a poster created that showed Senator Tydings as if in conversation with American Communist leader Earl Browder. The picture had been created from a composite of two separate photos — one of Tydings listening to the election returns of 1938 and the other showed Browder in 1950; and even though the caption indicated that it was a composite, the damage was done. Voters were turned. In defeat Tydings pointed out that "one picture is worth a thousand words."
2. Anna Ella Carroll
3. Oprah Winfrey portrayed herself on February 28, 1983.
4. Morrall joined the Giants in 1965 and left them for the Colts at the end of the 1967 season. He left Baltimore and played the 1972 season with the Miami Dolphins.
5. Tommy D'Alesandro, Jr.

Page 79:
1. "Bread and Butter" was used in the commercial — with some changes in wording.
2. Wally Orlinsky was at Allenwood Federal Penitentiary, Pennsylvania.
3. Joe Altobelli, manager of the Orioles
4. Henry Fonda was the actor; his wife was Margaret Sullavan.
5. Patterson Park across the Chesapeake

Page 80:
1. John Mackey who played nine years with the Colts
2. Lucas Brothers
3. Henrietta Haynie Maddox
4. Norman Thayer, Jr., portrayed by Henry Fonda, made the statement in the movie "On Golden Pond" which won Academy Awards.
5. The Battle Monument at North Calvert and Fayette Streets was constructed within the year following the close of the War of 1812 (which ended in 1814) and dedicated to those who died in the defense of the city. It is the first piece of architecture to be inspired by Egyptian works and is the first true battle or war memorial in the United States.

Page 81:
1. 1976
2. His name was James McHenry and he was the individual for whom the Star Fort was named: Fort McHenry. He had some indirect involvement in the planning and completion of the Whetstone Point fortification. Upon his death in 1816, McHenry was buried in Westminster Churchyard.
3. Spectacular Bid
4. Mencken was talking about the Chesapeake Bay.
5. "Eubie!"

Page 82:

1. Mayflower; fifteen vans
2. The Great Fort McHenry Bicycle Beer Race. The course is 1⅗-miles in length and the participants ride bikes from one stop to another, drinking an entire beer, without spilling a drop inside each tavern on the course.
3. Fussel, a milk dealer, used his surplus cream to manufacture ice cream, which was sold locally for $.60 per quart.
4. Agnew's campaign people borrowed the Cahn-Van Heusen song, "My Kind of Town, Chicago Is," to create: "My kind of man, Ted Agnew is."
5. Charles Carroll of Carrollton was the richest of all Signers of the Declaration of Independence and the wealthiest man in the United States when he died.

Page 83:

1. The letter was written by Frederick Douglass.
2. Rick Dempsey
3. Stan Stamenkovic of the Baltimore Blast was born in Yugoslavia, bought from the Memphis Americans for $150,000.
4. Two hundred twenty-eight
5. Independence Hall in Philadelphia, Pennsylvania

Page 84:

1. Brooks Robinson holds a lifetime record of hitting into 296 double plays.
2. Giacconi heads the Space Telescope Institute at Johns Hopkins University. (The Uhuru satellite was launched in 1970 and gave the world for the first time the ability to study X-rays from outer space in ways previously unavailable.)
3. Sportin' Life
4. The Republicans took on the name "Union Party" and called for a constitutional amendment outlawing slavery.
5. James Cardinal Gibbons, Archbishop of Baltimore

Page 85:

1. "Yankee, Yankee, remember the Maine!" The poem made reference to the explosion that tore through the battleship Maine on February 15, 1898, while moored in Havana harbor — and the killing of 260 officers and men. "Remember the Maine!" became a popular slogan of individuals who favored war with Spain over the incident.
2. Miles was hired to buy a cemetery plot for the Duke and Duchess in Greenmount Cemetery. The reason was that the Duke was refused burial in the royal family plot in England; later this was turned around by his mother, Queen Mary.
3. Baltimore is the only franchise to have a winning record against the New York Yankees.

4. "Saiontz & Kirk Think Irsay's A Jerk" was a reference to Robert Irsay's removal of the Baltimore Colts to Indianapolis in March of 1984.
5. Don Shula was the Colts coach.

Page 86:
1. Mona Freeman seen in such movies as "Black Beauty," "Mother Wore Tights," and "Battle Cry."
2. City Council wanted the United States to not attend the 1935 Olympic Games held that year in Berlin due to the anti-Semitic position held by Hitler and his government.
3. Rubber gloves
4. Saratoga and Holliday Streets
5. Virginia Poe had died at a very young age from the effects of consumption. She had met Poe while he was living with her family — after being kicked out of West Point; she was his cousin. At the time of their marriage, Virginia was 14. When she died in 1847, her only companion was a pet cat. Her remains were buried in a New York cemetery that years later was destroyed to make way for urban renewal. A close friend, William Gill, took what was left of her body, had the remains placed in a box which were then placed under his own bed in his home. For years the box was left there, until Virginia was delivered to Baltimore to join her husband in his second grave in Westminster Presbyterian Cemetery.

Page: 87
1. The Order of the Star-Spangled Banner
2. Stu Miller
3. Jonathan Hanson ran a flour mill in 1711.
4. Hicks appeared on "Tic Tac Dough" with Wink Martindale, winning $159,600. — the second highest ever on the TV quiz show.
5. The *Sun* story was a hoax created by H. L. Mencken — although the article was unsigned. The story told of the invention of the cocktail by John Henderson, a native of North Carolina and bartender at the hotel. As Mencken wrote it, Henderson made the first cocktail for Mr. Hopkins who had just been in a duel. Mencken revealed many of his fictional news stories in his autobiographical *Newspaper Days* published in 1941. The *Sun* article-hoax was entitled "The Secret History of the Cocktail."

Page 88
1. Jon Miller was the radio voice in Oakland, Texas, and Boston prior to joining his fourth American League city in 1983.
2. "Homewood" served as the home of the Country School for Boys — now known as Gilman School.
3. Marshall decided to study dentistry.
4. This big Baltimore product was used to make tents during the Civil War.
5. Airplanes
Page: 89
1. Sir Barton (1919), Gallant Fox (1930), Omaha (1935), War Admiral (1937), Whirlaway (1941)
2. Johnny Unitas in 1957 and 1967, Lenny Moore in 1964, and Earl Morrall in 1968

3. Right-hander Milt Pappas (1957–1965)
4. Pittsburgh Penguins
5. The Lacrosse Hall of Fame made its permanent home on the Homewood campus in 1963.
6. Philadelphia and Boston
7. New York Knicks
8. The Woodlawn Vase, created by Tiffany in 1860, when it's not being used for the Preakness
9. The Los Angeles Dodgers lost the World Series to the Orioles in 1966 — scoring only two runs. In that Series, Los Angeles didn't score one run after the third inning of the first game.
10. None

Page 90:

1. The Maryland Line Confederate Soldier's Home
2. Stephen A. Douglas ("The Little Giant") who became nationally famous for his 1858 debates with Lincoln
3. Ottmar Mergenthaler came from Germany. He invented the "linotype" and patented it in 1855. It revolutionized the printing industry, but was rejected by Baltimore newspapers because it might have put typesetters out of work. New York gets credit for its first use.
4. Mayor J. Harold Grady
5. Built in 1768, the first court house was later fitted with stilts made of masonry. The reason for the stilts was that Calvert Street was cut northward through a hill — upon which sat the court house. Many people of the day felt it presented the strangest sight of 18th-century Maryland.
6. Lincoln was talking of the defense of Washington, D.C.
7. Ireland
8. Jimmy Carter attended the Naval Academy at Annapolis.
9. General Billy Mitchell
10. It made no impression on him. He never saw Baltimore. He never crossed the Atlantic.

Page: 91

1. "A Funny Thing Happened on the Way to the Forum" was the last play at Ford's Theater. The building was torn down to make way for a parking lot.
2. The Milton S. Eisenhower Library at Johns Hopkins University
3. John Barth plots for (a) *Giles Goat-Boy,* (b) *Chimera,* and (c) *The Sot-Weed Factor.*
4. Daniel Mark Epstein
5. The students gave the zoo a portable black and white TV in an effort to raise spirits among the gorillas. It did not work.
6. Wally Orlinsky coordinated the cake project. It was shaped like the United States, floated on a barge in the inner harbor, attacked by rain and harbor rats.
7. Al Jolson
8. Peck portrayed F. (Francis) Scott Fitzgerald; Kerr played Sheila Graham.
9. "Minnie the Moocher"
10. Stein's autobiobraphy was entitled, *The Autobiography of Alice B. Toklas.*

Page: 92

1. Brooks Robinson
2. Robert Moses "Lefty" Grove who specialized in the fastball was known as a one-pitch pitcher.
3. Satchel Paige
4. Babe Ruth
5. Jim Palmer
6. Mike Flanagan was "Cy Young;" Stone was "Cy Present;" Jim Palmer was "Cy Past;" Scott McGregor was "Cy Future;" and Dennis Martinez was "Cy Future Future."
7. Frank Robinson
8. Jim Hartzell created and drew the "Oriole." Mark Wauben was the next to draw it.
9. Baltimore beat the Boston Red Sox 3–2
10. Billy "Digger" O'Dell

Page: 93

1. 1784
2. 1957; it is 7,650 feet long under the Patapsco River.
3. 1928
4. Excelsiors
5. The Order of Odd Fellows
6. 1949
7. 1776
8. 1916
9. 1977
10. Charles Carroll of Carrollton

Page: 94

1. Allegre tied the record held by Lou Michaels in a game which saw the Colts defeat the Eagles 22–21.
2. The Bloomfield Rams (Pennsylvania); rumor has it that Johnny may have made as much as $7.00 per game.
3. Jim Parker
4. Don Ellison
5. Jones made 17 consecutive passes against the Jets.
6. Lenny Moore made the winning TD (75 yards) to help beat the San Francisco 49ers.
7. Kevin Rutledge
8. 1972; 1977 was the year of biggest attendance figures — 385,864.
9. Lenny Moore
10. Wilbur "Weeb" Eubank

Page: 95

1. Bold Champeau (1975, 8th), Bold Ego (1981, 2nd), Bold Reason (1971, 5th), Bold Ruler (1957, 1st), Bold Style (1982, 4th), Bold Venture (1936, 1st)

2. Bimelech was the first to wear the floral horseshoe. Prior to 1940 a blanket of roses was draped over the winner's withers.
3. Richard M. Nixon, then the vice president
4. He won three and never failed to finish in the money in the remainder. Arcaro rode in fifteen events of the years, finishing in the money on twelve occasions.
5. A question mark
6. Flocarline won in 1903; Whimsical in 1906, Rhine Maiden in 1915, and Nellie Morse in 1924.
7. Assault ridden by Eddie Arcaro
8. Sunday
9. The Dixie Handicap, Pimlico Oaks, Jennings Handicap, and the Pimlico Nursery
10. The Belmont (1867), the Preakness (1873), the Kentucky Derby (1875)

Page: 96

1. The registration number of a private plane that crashed into the second deck of Memorial Stadium on December 19, 1976 following a game between the Colts and the Steelers. The plane was piloted by David N. Kroner, a former undercover drug agent.
2. Roday took credit for enlarging the breasts of his clients and having an 80 percent retention of size.
3. Edith Massey started these groups — of which "Poobah" was her beginnings into punk rock. Massey, known to many as "The Egg Lady," has starred with musical groups, has tended bar at The Full Moon Saloon, and a part of the John Waters clique.
4. Klaus Wagner
5. This was the amount of the check (and its date and number) handed over by Spiro Agnew to the State of Maryland in repayment for alleged bribes. This made the total paid back $432,500.00. The check was drawn on the Bank of America.
6. Name given to Baltimore's first radar/computer system for traffic control. Henry A. Barnes was traffic director since 1953 and left for New York City.
7. Baltimore Oriole Mike Flanagan
8. J. R. "Reg" Murphy of the Sunpapers
9. Judge John Pratt (1st trial) and Judge Robert Taylor (2nd trial). Barnet Skolnik was the chief prosecutor.
10. Baltimore Experimental High School

Page: 97

1. Eddie Danna at the Tower Barber Shop (East Baltimore Street)
2. 1944
3. The Episcopal Church
4. Daniel Berrigan said these lines in Saul Levitt's "The Trial of the Catonsville Nine."
5. Governor Oden Bowie
6. Riverview Amusement Park
7. David W. Chambers was Whittaker Chambers, the man who told a House of Representatives committee that Alger Hiss was responsible for espionage.

8. Mike Boddicker; the "fosball" is a hybrid created by a mixture of a fork ball and a "fish" (Philadelphia pitching coach, Claude Osteen, coined the term for a changeup).
9. The chambers were in a wax museum. The movie was later adapted into a play that had a run in Baltimore at The Mechanic.
10. George Gipe

Page: 98
1. George Washington
2. SURRENDER was the headline of the May 7, 1945 *Evening Sun,* announcing the surrender of Japan and the end of World War II.
3. Andrew Jackson made the trip in 1833; it was three miles long.
4. CPR (Coronary Pulmonary Resuscitation)
5. Mencken was making reference to Aileen Pringle, a silent movie star he had dated in the 1920's.
6. If you said Enoch Pratt, you are wrong. It was George Peabody in 1866.
7. Charles, Baltimore and Calvert Streets
8. John Adams on June 15, 1800
9. They were given the right to construct a private telephone system in the city — The Maryland Telephone Company.
10. Christopher Columbus

Page: 99
1. Eleven turnovers: five fumbles and six interceptions
2. George Andrie hit Unitas; Earl Morrall replaced him.
3. Jim O'Brien kicked the game winning 32-yard field goal.
4. The "cat" was Jim Brown. After the game, Lipscomb said: "I'm still waiting to get my hands on that cat."
5. Woody Hayes at Ohio State
6. Lenny Moore
7. Raymond Berry came to the Colts from Southern Methodist University; he retired in 1967.
8. Bruce Laird
9. Don Joyce
10. Keith Molesworth was named coach in 1953; he shifted to chief talent scout in 1954. The shift paid off in 1954, when 12 rookies were put on the roster including: George Shaw, Alan Ameche, L. G. Dupre, Jack Patera, George Preas, and Dick Szymanski (all became regulars).

Page: 100
1. A ball that once hit takes a very high bounce in the infield. It is thought that it had been purposely used by John McGraw (its inventor) and "Wee Willie" Keeler when both played for the Orioles in the 1890's. McGraw played 3rd base (1891–1895).
2. Duke Ellington (1899–1974), who had been christened Edward Kennedy Ellington
3. The lot number he was buried in — "80"

4. These children formed a human flag, wearing red, white and blue caps, at Fort McHenry. It was a 100 foot by 60 foot interpretation of the Star-Spangled Banner.
5. Sugar Ray fought and defeated Luis "The Bull" Vega. The day before the fight, he took his son (Ray, Jr.) to see the movie "Rocky."
6. Henry Clay
7. Redwood Street
8. Eleven
9. Chris Hinton
10. By the early 19th century, Baltimore had become the shipbuilding center of the nation. In 1814 the city was building the Baltimore Flyer and in 1823 the famous Baltimore Clipper was gaining popularity. Clipper came from "clip" an English word meaning "trim, shipshape" about 1710. By 1820 the word was being used in America to mean "to move fast." However, the sailing ship described in the question was the Baltimore Schooner. These ships of two to seven masts were popular in the United States and in Canada until the middle of the 19th century. They were fast, sleek ships that gave the impression that they skimmed across the surface of the water — just like a stone. The game children play with flat stones is called "scooning."

Index

A

"A Funny Thing Happened on the Way to the Forum," 91
A Survival Guide for the Bedeviled Male, 20
Abell, Arunah Shepherdson, 78
Acuff, Roy, 33
Accorsi, Ernie, 24, 74
Adams, John, 81, 98
Adams, John Quincy, 42
Agnew, Spiro T., 3, 16, 36, 57, 75, 82, 96
Agnus, Felix, 65
Albert, Carl, 44
Alex Brown and Sons, 13, 90
Allegre, Raul, 94
Allenwood Federal Penitentiary, 79
Altobelli, Joe, 79
Ameche, Alan, 99
"American Revolutionary Army," 53
American Turf Register and Sporting Magazine, 48
Anderson, John, 73
Anderson, Maxwell, 24
Andrie, George, 99
Arcaro, Eddie, 10, 95
Argonaut, 34
Armstrong, Bess, 7, 72
Arnold, Samuel, 57, 72
Arthur, Timothy S., 14
"Artist, The," 19
Asbury, Francis, 66
Asheville, North Carolina, 9
Asquith, Colonel Hobart, 25
Assault, 95
Atlanta Constitution, 53
Austin, Gene, 1
Autobiography of Alice B. Toklas, 91

B

Babe Ruth's Home Run Candy, 46
Bachelor's Cotillion, 71
Bailey, John T., 16
Baker, Russell, 39
Ballistics, 28
Balloon flight, 93
Baltimore:
 and Norfolk Steam Packet Company, 12
 and Ohio Railroad, 9, 11, 18, 42, 49, 50, 73
 Banners, 17
 Blast, 32, 38, 64, 83
 Blues, 18
 Bullets, 3, 78, 89
 City Certificates, 62
 City College, 43
 Civic Center, 7, 100
 Clay, 6
 Clippers, 100
 Colts (see Colts)
 Cotton Duck Extra, 88
 Dental College, 59
 Elite Giants, 59
 Excelsiors, 93
 Experimental High School, 96
 Fire Department, 98
 Harbor Tunnel, 93
 Law School, 80
 Museum of Art, 29, 38, 64, 89
 Oriole, 66
 Orioles, 1, 3, 5, 8, 9, 10, 13, 15, 16, 17, 19, 20, 23, 27, 31, 33, 35, 39, 40, 47, 48, 50, 54, 55, 56, 57, 60, 61, 67, 69, 70, 71, 72, 74, 75, 76, 77, 79, 80, 81, 83, 84, 85, 87, 88, 89, 92, 96, 97, 100
 Polytechnic Institute, 10
 Postal system, 70
 Ravens, 50
 Skipjacks, 89
 Symphony, 93
 Town, 87
 Washington International Airport, 55
 Yellow Stockings, 16
Baltimore's Best, 35
Baltimore Business Journal, 68
Baseball:
 Bacharach Giants, 59
 Excelsiors, 16, 93
 Federal League Terrapins, 16
 Lord Baltimores, 16
 Marylands, 16
 Orioles, (See Baltimore)
 Pastime, 16
Bannecker, Benjamin, 43, 46, 66
Banks, Nathaniel P., 77
Barne's Brain, 96
Barnes, Ernie, 6
Barnum and Bailey's Circus, 73
Barnum's City Hotel, 72
Barnum, David, 72
Barnum, P. T., 52
Barth, John, 40, 45
Basilica of the Assumption, 4, 34
Basketball, 39, 46, 50
Battle Cry, 69
Battle Monument, 80
Bauer, Hank, 27
Beam, George, 16
Beall, J. Glenn, 78
Beatles, 7
Beauregard, Pierre G. T., 81
Bee Bee Bee, 14
Behaviorism, 13
Bel Air, 6
"Believe It or Not," 15, 41
Belvedere Hotel, 31, 49, 62, 73
Belmont Stakes, 95
Berman, Edgar, M.D., 20
Berrigan, Daniel, 7, 97
Berrigan, Philip, 7
Berry, Raymond, 30, 99
Bethlehem-Fairfield shipyards, 48
"Betty Betterspeech," 17
Bicentennial cake, 91
Bickford, Charles, 43
Bimelech, 95
Birneys, 30
Black Aggie, 65
Black, Van-Lear, 25
Black-eyed susans, 95
Blair, Paul, 5
Blake, Eubie, 48, 58, 77
Blalock, Alfred, 50
Blanda, George, 62
Blaustein, Jacob, 25
Block, The, 2, 15, 33, 46, 57, 77
Bloomfield Rams, 94
Bloody Inks, 16
Bloody Tubs, 16
Blue babies, 50
Boddicker, Mike, 19, 97
Bodie, Ping, 70
"Bohemian," 68
Bold, 10
Bold Bidder, 81
Bold Champeau, 95
Bold Ego, 95
Bold Reason, 95
Bold Ruler, 10, 95
Bold Style, 95
Bold Venture, 95
Bolton Station, 83
Bolus River, 8
Bonaparte, Jerome, 63
Bonaparte, Napoleon, 63
Bonheur Memorial Park, 6
Bonner, Lee, 35
Booth Edwin, 22
Booth, John Wilkes, 6, 22, 34, 57, 72, 74, 86
Booth, Junius Brutus, 6
Booth, Junius Brutus, Jr., 86
Bowling, 27
Bowie, Odin, 97

Bozo the Clown, 73
Brady, "Diamond Jim," 51
Brannum, Hugh, 63
Brasse, Ordell, 37
Brills, 30
Brenner, Stephen, 73
Broening, William F., 7, 41
Bromo Seltzer, 13, 29, 46
Brother Mathias, 43
Browder, Earl, 78
Brown, James, 3
Brown, Jim, 94, 99
Brown, John, 51
Brown, Kenneth, 59
Brown vs. Board of Education, 31
Brown's Wharf, 90
Bryn Mawr School, 31
Buchanan, James, 67
Bugeyes, 26
Bumbry, Al, 47
Bunting, Dr., 11
Burger, Robert, 5
Bushman, Francis X., 5, 64
Butler, Benjamin, 87

C
Cadwell,, Joe, 3
Calhoun, James, 32
California, 1, 4
Calloway, Cab, 14, 91
Calvert, George, 18
Calvert Hall, 75
Cambridge Arms Apartments, 4
Camden Station, 83
Campanella, Roy, 59
Candy Spots, 25
Canton, 24, 41
Captain Kangaroo, 63
Carmichael, Hoagy, 26
Carpathia, 88
Carroll, Anna Ella, 78
Carroll, Charles (of Carrollton), 4, 42,
    47, 72, 73, 82, 88, 93
Carroll, James, 42
Carroll, John, 11, 22
Carroll Mansion, 4
Carry Back, 83
Carter, Jimmy, 53, 65, 90, 96
Carter, William E., 88
Cary, Constance, 81, 87
Cary, Hetty, 81, 87
Cary, Jennie, 35, 81
Cassavetes, John, 11
Caton Iron Works, 9
Catonsville Nine, 7
Caucici, Henrico, 28
Chambers, David, W., 97
Chambers, Whittaker, 72, 97
"Championship 10," 12
Chappelle, Howard, 24
Charles I, 40

Charles Center, 62, 90
Charles, Nick, 60
Charles Street, 1
Checkers Speech, 76
Chesapeake, 53
Chesapeake and Ohio Railroad, 23, 32
Chessie, 32
"Chevy Chase," 48
CIA, 5
Citation, 10, 21, 95
City College, 69
City Paper, The, 64, 79
City Squeeze, The, 64
Civic Center, 7, 93, 100
Civil War, 11, 12,
Claggetts' Brewery, 40
Clay, Henry, 40, 100
Cleopatra's Needle, 12
Cleveland, Grover, 46
Cloisters, The, 39
C&O Canal, 42
Cockpit Street, 10
Cocktail, 87
Codex, 31
Cohen, Mendes I., 82
Cole's Harbor, 61
Colored High School, 85
Colosseum, 37
Colts, 2, 6, 9, 12, 21, 24, 29, 30, 32, 36,
    41, 42, 43, 44, 45, 49, 52, 53, 55,
    57, 62, 63, 64, 68, 69, 73, 74, 78,
    80, 82, 85, 89, 94, 99, 100
Columbia Iron Works and Drydock
    Company, 34
"Columbiad," 54
Columbus, Christopher, 98
Commissiona, Sergui, 68
Compleat Chauvinist, 20
Cone, Claribel, 64
Cone, Etta, 64
Congreve rockets, 11
Constellation Question, The, 24
Constellation, United States Frigate, 24,
    41, 60, 75, 98
Constitution, United States, 1
Content, 47
Cooper, Kenny, 38
Cooper, Peter, 9, 50
Corbett, "Gentleman Jim," 8, 50
Corbett, Joe, 8
Cordero, Angel, 31
Cornish, Harry, 29
Coronary Pulmonary Resuscitation, 98
Cowley, Malcolm, 79
Cowley, R. Adams, 49
Crabs, 17
Cricket, Jiminy, 33
Cross Keys, 54
Crown Cork and Seal Company, 82
Cruz, Todd, 61
Cuozzo, Gary, 2
Curtin, Valerie, 72, 74
Cy Young Award, 92

D
D'Alesandro, Tommy, Jr., 78
Daily Racing Form, 42
Dalkowski, Steve, 3
Damascus, 25, 75
Dandy, Walter, 9, 19
Dark-horse, 45
Darin, Bobby, 67
Dauer, Rich, 61
Daughters of Charity, 75
Davidge Hall, 7
Davis, Augustus C., 98
De Boy, David, 12
DeCinces, Doug, 70
Declaration of Independence, 47, 73, 82,
    93
Democrats, 45, 52, 55, 66, 67, 68, 74,
    78, 90
Dempsey, Rick, 61, 83
Denver Boot, 59
Designated Hitters, 74
Devine, Catherine, 52
Dickens, Charles, 72
Dietrich, Marlene, 68
Dobson, Tamara, 28
Donaldson, Walter, 1
Donovan, Art, 37
Dos Passos, Jon, 9, 54, 68
Doughty, Glenn, 69
Douglas, Stephen A., 90
Douglass, Frederick, 26, 77, 83
Douglass High School, 14, 74
Drabowsky, Moe, 39
Dracula, 17
Dreiser, Theodore, 15, 68
Drew, John, 71
Druid Hill, 16
Dundalk, 3, 73, 81
Dunne, Jack, 55
Dupre, L. G., 99
Dykes, Jimmy, 40, 48

E
Earp, Wyatt, 59
Edgar, The, 54
Edgar Allan Poe Award, 76
Edwards, Cliff, 33
Eisenbrandt, Christian, 50
Eisenhower, Milton, 73, 75, 91
Ellicott, Andrew, 66
Ellicott, Joseph, 66
Ellicott Mills, 98
Elliott, "Mama" Cass, 60
Ellington, Duke, 75, 100
Ellison, Don, 94
Ellsworth, Annie, 56
Elway, John, 100
End of the Road, 45
"Enfants Terrible," 96
Epstein, Daniel Mark, 91
Eubank, Wilbur, "Weeb," 94

"Eubie," 81
Eutaw, 34
Evans, Damon, 74
Exodus, 37

F
Facedancer, 33
Fahlberg, Constantine, 16
Fallon, George H., 52
Farrow, Mia, 11
Federal Hill, 1
Fells Point, 22, 26, 52, 90
Fells Point Diner, 8
Ferber, Edna, 43
Fillmore, Millard, 54, 68, 87
Finney, John M. T., 78
Fireman Award, 87
Fisher, Dr. Russell S., 12
Fitzgerald, Ella, 31
Fitzgerald, F. Scott, 4, 45, 48, 56, 67,
    70, 79
Fitzgerald, Zelda Sayre, 48, 67, 79
"Fizz Water," 48
Flag, 7, 21, 40, 65, 81, 93, 98, 100
Flag Admiral, 65
Flanagan, Mike, 92, 96
Flanagan, Robert, 73
Flapper, 71
Fleming, Fanny Belle, 2
Flocarline, 47, 95
Foch, Nina, 23
Fonda, Henry, 79, 80
Fonda, Jane, 70
Fool Brothers, The, 12
Football:
    Colts (see Colts)
Ford's Theater, 85, 91
Foreman, Avon, 7
Forest Park High School, 17
Forsythe, John, 31, 40
Fort Armistead, 57
Fort Carroll, 57
Fort McHenry, 8, 11, 21, 25, 28, 40, 42,
    44, 59, 61, 65, 71, 77, 93, 100
Fosball, 97
Francis Scott Key Memorial, 25
Franklin, Rhea, 17
Franklin, Ronnie, 3, 81
"Free Lance, The," 30
Freeman, Mona, 86
Frenkil, Victor, 49
"Friendly Fire," 79
Friendship International Airport, 55
Frisby, Herbert M., 47
From the Earth to the Moon, 54
Fuld brothers, 45
Fuselage Avenue, 10
Fussel, Jacob, 82

G
Gail, Pam, 46
Gallant Fox, 89
Galt, Edith Bolling, 67
Gambling, 58
Gardner, Erle Stanley, 12, 44
Garret, Mary, 38
Garrett, Robert, 4
Garrison, William Lloyd, 12
Gas Light Company, 44
Gentile, Jim, 20, 69
Genuine Risk, 31, 47
Gershwin, George, 19
Giancconi, Riccardo, 84
Gibbons, James Cardinal, 84
Gifford, Frank, 49
Gilman School, 88
Gipe, George, 97
Glenn L. Martin Company, 10, 36, 88
Go Go's, 14
Goddard, William, 70
Goldsborough, William Worthington, 62
Goode, Wilson, 18
Gorsuch, Charles, 42
Gorsuch Point, 36
Goucher College, 36
Grady, J. Harold, 78, 90
Graf Zeppelin, 93
Graham, Sheilah, 91
Grammer, G. Edward, 49
Gray Ghost, 51
"Grease," 17
Great Fire of 1904, 13, 27, 30, 40, 65
Great Fort McHenry Bicycle Beer Race,
    82
Great Western Champagne, 72
Greenmount Cemetery, 34, 85
Grey, Dillon, 72
Grimsley, Ross, 77
Grove, Robert Moses "Lefty," 92
Guinness Book of World Records, 3, 91,
    96
Gun Club of Baltimore, 54
Gunther, Henry, 41

H
Hadassah, 19
Haldeman, H. R., 24
Halsted, William S., 86
Hamilton, Edith, 31
Hammen, Donald, 33
Hammett, Dashiell, 44, 60
Hansen, Ron, 57
Hanson, Jonathan, 87
Harbor Field, 28
Harding, Warren G., 24, 25
Hare, Joseph Thompson, 4
Harper's Ferry, 51, 62, 83
Harrisburg, Pennsylvania, 23
Hart, Gary, 66

Hartigan, Grace, 13
Hartman, David, 10
Hartzell, Jim, 92
Haussner's Restaurant, 39
Hawaii, 28
Hayden, Tom, 70
Head, Howard, 36
Hecht Department Store, 24
Heco, Joseph, 82
Hellman, Andrew, 49
Hemingway, Ernest, 58, 70
Henderson, John Welby, 87
Henry, John, 23
Henry, Joseph, 56
Henson, Matthew, 47
Hiawatha, 5
Hicks, Wilbur, 87
Highlandtown, 51
Hill Prince, 10
Hinckley, John, 69
Hinton, Chris, 64, 100
Hinton, Eddie, 19
Hippie High, 96
Hirchberg, Leonard, 68
Hirsch, Judd, 61
Hiss, Alger, 72
Hitchcock, Alfred, 40
Holliday, John Henry "Doc," 59
Holloway, Mrs. Reuben Ross, 15
Holmes, Oliver Wendell, 58
"Home of the Brave," 56
Homewood, 88, 89
Homewood Field, 82
"Homo boobiens," 67
Hooker, 22
Hoover, Herbert, 67, 92
Hopkins, Charles, 30
Hopkins, John A., 87
Hopkins, Johns, 29
Hopkins Place Savings Bank, 65
"Hot l Baltimore," 46, 61
"Hot Rats," 63
Horn, Adam, 49
Houston Summit, 32
Howard, John Eager, 34
Howard, Joseph, 23
Howard's Park, 93
Hunter, Jim "Catfish," 35

I
"I Wonder Park," 41
"Incredible Edible Eggs," 96
Independence Hall, 83
Ireland, 23, 90
Irsay, Jimmy, 21
Irsay, Robert, 45, 68, 82, 85, 94

J
Jackson, Andrew, 18, 74, 98
Jackson, Jesse, 66

Jackson, Reggie, 5, 33, 35, 63
Jackson, Thomas J. ("Stonewall"), 55
James Adams Floating Theatre, 43
"Jenny and the Phoenix," 91
Jewison, Norman, 74
John Eager Howard Room, 73
Johns Hopkins Hospital, 9, 19, 35, 50,
    51, 69, 86, 98
Johns Hopkins University, The, 3, 5,
    13, 16, 20, 50, 53, 58, 59, 69, 72,
    75, 82, 84, 88, 89, 91
Johnson, Andrew, 86
Johnson, Lyndon B., 53
Johnson, Walter, 92
Jolson, Al, 91
Jones, Bert, 45, 53, 94
Jones, Cleon, 76
Joplin, Janis, 9
Joppy, 83
Joyce, Don, 99
Jungle, The, 47
Jungle Band, 75

K
Kaline, Al, 71
Kauai King, 83
Keach, Stacy, 45
Keeler, Wee Willie, 67, 100
Kelly, Gene, 23, 32
Kelly, "Shipwreck," 7
Kempski, Sandy, 91
Kennedy, John F., 24
Kennedy, John P., 14, 73
Kensett, Thomas, 69
Kernan, James L., 52
Kernan's Dining Room, 79
Kerr, John, 39
Key, Francis Scott, 7, 11, 15, 33, 37, 42,
    55, 79, 97
Key, Philip Barton, 42
Kilrain, Jake, 50
Knickerbocker Club, 29
Know-Nothing Party, 68
Kopits, Steven E., 35
Kramer, Stanley, 56
Kroner, Donald N., 96
Kush, Frank, 21, 29, 94

L
La Cosa Nostra, 8
Lacks, Henrietta, 69
Lacrosse Hall of Fame, 89
Lady of the Lake, 26
Laird, Bruce, 99
Lake, Simon, 34
Lamont, Jackie, 46
Lamour, Dorothy, 48
Lampe, Sam, 46
"Last Mile, The," 79

Last Time When, The, 97
Latrobe, Benjamin, 34, 36
Laurent, Arthur, 56
Lazaretto Light, 36
Lear, Norman, 6, 46
Lee, Robert E., 51, 55, 57
L'Enfant, Pierre, 66
Leonard, Sugar Ray, 100
Leone, Dominic A., 30
Levinson, Barry, 72
Lexington Market, 93
Liberty ships, 48
Lighthouse, The, 36
Lincoln, Abraham, 22, 23, 36, 45, 48,
    57, 72, 74, 77, 78, 86, 90
Lincoln, Robert, 22
Lind, Bob, 27
Linnaeus, Carolus, 66
Lipscomb, Big Daddy, 32, 49, 99
Little Big Horn, 76
Little Egypt, 52
Little Tavern Shop, The, 34
Littlepage's Furniture, 5
Long, Avon, 84
Long, Clarence, 75
Long, Governor Earl, 2, 24
Long, Huey, 34
Longfellow, Henry Wadsworth, 5
Lord Baltimore, 66, 90
"lost generation," 70
Loudon Park Cemetery, 6, 25, 32, 60,
    62, 76
Lovely Lane, 66
LSD, 5, 22
Lucas Brothers, 80

M
Mackey, John, 19, 80
Maddox, Henrietta Haynie, 80
Madison, Dolley, 33
Madison, James, 33
Mafia, 8
Magruder, John Bankhead ("Prince
    John"), 55
Male Central High School, 43
Manchester, Melissa, 29
Mandel, Marvin, 96
Mann, Andrea, 44
Marchebroda, Ted, 99
Marchetti, Gino, 49
Marshall, John, 47
Marshall, Thurgood, 14, 31, 88
Martin, Billy, 50
Martin, Steve, 97
Martinez, Dennis, 92
Maryland Institute, 48
Maryland Institute for Emergency Med-
    ical Medicine, 49
Maryland Jockey Club, 71, 93, 95, 97
Maryland Line Confederate Soldiers'
    Home, 90

*Maryland Line in the Confederate States
    Army, The,* 62
Maryland Polo Club, 82
Maryland State Penitentiary, 59, 79
Maryland Telephone Company, 98
Massey, Edith, 14, 96
Master derby, 83
Masters, Edgar Lee, 2
Mathias, Charles, Jr., 61
Matisse, Henri, 64
Matte, Tom, 2, 99
Mays, Dorothy, 21
Maximilian, 55
McCarthy, Joe, 78
McComas, Henry, 14
McCormack, Mike, 69
McCormick and Company, 4
McCulloch, James, 47
McCulloch vs. Maryland, 47
McGlennen, James, 65
McGraw, John, 67, 100
McGregor, Scott, 92
McGuffy Reader, 14
McHenry, James, 81
McLane, Mayor, 42
McLane, Robert Milligan, 76
McNally, Dave, 1, 35
McQuade, Bud, 75
Medora, 12
Memorial Stadium, 31, 85, 96
Mencken, Henry L., 2, 6, 15, 17, 19, 28,
    32, 38, 45, 54, 56, 67, 68, 71, 81,
    87, 98
Mergenthaler, Ottmar, 90
Merryman, John, 77
METROS, 46
Meyerhoff, Harry, 3, 81
Meyerhoff, Joseph, 20
Michaels, Lou, 94
Mikulski, Barbara, 44
Miles, Clarence, 85
Milford Mill High School, 32
Miller, Jon, 88
Miller, Stu, 87
Mills, Robert, 51
Milton Academy, 6
Milton Inn, 6
Mind Over Meter, 16
Minden, 33
Mitchell, Billy, 90
Mitchell, Clarence, Jr., 58, 66
Mitchell, Margaret, 45
MK-ULTRA, 5
Molesworth, Keith, 99
Molineux, Roland, 29
Mondale, Walter, 66
Mondawmin, 5
Monday German, 71
Monroe, Earle, 3, 78
Monument Street landfill, 51
Moore, Garry, 54
Moore Lenny, 9, 30, 89, 94, 99
Moore, Thomas, 82

Morgan State, 18
Morley, Christopher, 53
Morrall, Earl, 78, 89, 99
Morse, Samuel F., 56, 100
Moss, Howie, 97
Moss, Hunter, 20
Moth-Eaten Mink, 12
Motion Pictures:
  "An American in Paris," 23
  "And Justice for All," 31, 74
  "Animal House," 1, 72
  "Battle Cry," 86
  "Beloved Infidel," 91
  "Best Friends," 72
  "Chamber of Horrors," 97
  "Cleopatra Jones," 28
  "Diner," 8, 34, 68, 72, 86
  "Gone With the Wind," 45
  "Grease," 17
  "Headin' Home," 27
  "Inherit the Wind," 32
  "Kitty Foyle," 53
  "On Golden Pond," 80
  "Ordinary People," 61
  "Pink Flamingos," 72
  "Raiders of the Lost Ark," 72
  "Rocky," 100
  "Rosemary's Baby," 11
  "The Babe Comes Home," 27, 37
  "The Babe Ruth Story," 43
  "The Devil is a Woman," 68
  "The House on Sorority Row," 72
  "The Ninth Inning," 37
  "The Pride of the Yankees," 37
  "To Have and Have Not," 26
  "Topaz," 40
  "Two for the Money," 35
  "Two Minute Warning," 12
Mount Clare, 72
Mount Clare Station, 56
Mount Vernon Place, 93
Mr. Greenjeans, 63
Mudd, Samuel, 57
Murdock, David, 24
Murphy, James, Jr., 52
Murphy, Reg, 53, 96
Murray, Eddie, 9, 54
Murray, Jim, 65
Murray, Madalyn (O'Hare), 19
Murray, Ray, 48
Murrow, Edward R., 11, 56
Mussolini, Benito, 57
Mutton, Jim, 30

N
N6276J, 96
Narrative of A. Gordon Pym, The, 51
Nash, Ogden, 25, 41, 56
Nashua, 10
Native Dancer, 51, 83

National Bohemian, 11
Naval Academy, 90
Needle, Karen, 32
Nellie Morse, 47, 95
New Yorker, The, 41
Newman, Randy, 6
News American, 29, 59
News-Post, 69
Newspaper Days, 87
Nicknames, 48
Nixon, Richard M., 1, 24, 72, 76, 78, 95
Nobel Prize for Peace, 59
North Point, 14
North Pole, 47
Noxzema, 11

O
Oasis, 46
O'Brian, Jim, 99
O'Dell, Billy "Digger," 92
O'Laughlin, Michael, 57
Olson, Dr. Frank, 5
Olympics, 4, 86
Omaha, 89
Order of Odd Fellows, 93
Order of the Star-Spangled Banner, 87
Orioles. (SEE BASEBALL)
Orlinsky, Walter, 76, 79, 91
Orr, Jimmy, 63
Osler, Sir William, 20
Ouija board, 45
Owings, Mr., 21

P
Pacino, Al, 31
Paige, Satchel, 92
Painter, William, 82
Palm Room, 73
Palmer, Jim, 35, 43, 92
Paper coins, 62
Papp, Joseph, 91
Pappas, Milt, 89
Parker Estate, 39
Parker, Jim, 94
Patapsco, 8, 14, 93
Patera, Jack, 99
Patrick Henry, 48
Patterson, Betsy, 63
Patterson Park, 79
Payne, Lewis, 74
Peabody, George, 98
Peabody Institute, The, 11
Peale, Rembrandt, 44
Peary, Robert E., 47
Peck, Gregory, 91
Pellington, Bill, 37
Peter Witts, 30
Peters, Hank, 81
Picasso, 58

Pickersgill, Mary, 40, 93
Pierce, Franklin, 55, 60
Pimlico, 25, 26, 27, 49, 63, 72, 78, 81
Pimlico Nursery, 95
Pimlico Oaks, 95
Pimlico Special, 21, 26
Pinkerton, Allan, 23
Pinkerton Detective Agency, 44
Playboy, 21, 44
Plimpton, George, 36
Poe, Edgar Allan, 2, 14, 15, 20, 30, 36, 46, 51, 62, 73, 76, 81, 84–85, 100
Poe, Virginia, 86
Poems:
  "The Defense of Fort McHenry," 15
Polhemus, Henry, 16
"Politian," 36
Political gangs, 16
Polk, James, 10, 45
Polland, Leon, 24
Polynesian, 83
Ponselle, Rosa, 40, 64
Pony Express, 58
Pope Leo XIII, 84
Pope Paul VI, 75
Pope Pius VII, 63
Post, Emily, 65
Powell, Boog, 15
Pratt, Enoch, 98
Pratt, John, 96
Preakness, 63
Preakness, 3, 10, 14, 22, 25, 31, 38, 42, 47, 49, 52, 63, 65, 66, 74, 75, 78, 79, 81, 83, 89, 95
Preakness Festival Balloon Race, 79
Preas, George, 99
President Warfield, 37
Presley, Elvis, 93
Price, T. Rowe, 26
Pride of Baltimore, 4
Prince Philip, 10
Pringle, Aileen, 98
Professional Amateur, The, 36
Propeller Drive, 10
Pungies, 26

R
Radcliffe, 3
Radio City Music Hall, 29
Raimondi's Florist, 22
Ralston, Dr., 80
Ralston Health Club, 80
Randal, James Ryder, 35
Randall, Tony, 20
Reagan, Ronald, 69
Regret, 31
Reiner, Carl, 97
Remsen, Ira, 16
Renfield, Mr., 21
Republican Party, 1, 84
Rhine Maiden, 47, 95

Richards, Paul, 92
Rickey, Branch, 59
Ripken, Cal, Jr., 60
Ripley, Robert, 15
Ripps, Lenny, 45
Riverview Amusement Park, 97
Robinson, Bill "Bojangles," 73
Robinson, Brooks, 10, 18, 84, 92
Robinson, Frank, 17, 20, 89, 92
"Rock Hard Peter," 96
Roday, James, 96
Rogers, Ginger, 53
Rogers, Mary, 84
Roget, Marie, 85
Rolling Stones, 10
"Romper Room", 2
Roosevelt, Alice, 27
Roosevelt, Franklin, 25, 33
Roosevelt, Mrs. Franklin D., 46
Roosevelt, Teddy, 27, 80
Rosenbloom, Carroll, 99
Rosman, Mark, 72
Ross, Betsy, 40
Ross, General Robert, 14
Rouse, James, 20
Rozelle Rule, 80
Russo, Jim, 19
Ruth, Babe, 18, 27, 29, 33, 37, 43, 46,
    55, 70, 73, 92
Rutledge, Kevin, 94

S
Saccharin, 16
Safire, William, 3
Saggy, 83
Saint Francis Xavier Church, 16, 44
Saint Helen, John, 86
Saint Mary's Academy, 33
Saint Mary's Industrial School, 43, 70,
    91
Saint Timothy's Hall, 57
Saiontz & Kirk, 85
Salsbury, Julius "Lord," 46
Sample, Johnny, 73
San Francisco, 4
Saturday Visitor, The, 73
Schaefer, Donald, 39, 53, 97
Scherr, Nathan, 64
Schmidt, Carl, 27
Schmidt's Blue Ribbon Bread, 79
Schnellenberger, Howard, 42
Schooners, 26
Schultz, Dwight, 75
Schwartz, Arthur, 64
Scott, General Winfield, 48
Scott, Sir Walter, 14, 26
Scrod, 55
Seabiscuit, 26
Secretariat, 74
Seton, Elizabeth Ann Bayley, 75
Seven Stars Tavern, 93

Shapiro, Ron, 63
Shaw, George, 55, 73, 99
Sheppard-Pratt Hospital, 48, 67
Shinnick, Don, 73
Shock, Gina, 14
Shoemaker, Willie, 25
Shot Tower, 36
Show Boat, 43
"Shuffle Along," 77, 81
Shula, Don, 63, 85
Sicles, Dan, 42
Simpson, Wallis Warfield, 15, 47
Sinclair, Upton, 47, 93
Singleton, Ken, 54
Sir Barton, 42, 89
Skolnik, Barnet, 96
Slavery, 12, 21, 84
Smith, Bessie, 9
Smith, Captain John, 8
Smith, Holden, 29
Smith, Red, 59
Smith, Sam, 63
Smithsonian, 21, 43, 65
Snodgrass, Dr. J. E., 30
Soccer, 21, 38
    Baltimore Blast, 32, 38, 64, 83, 89
"Son of Mr. Green Genes," 63
Songs and recordings:
    "About Face," 33
    "Anacreontic Song," 37
    "Baltimore, Md., That's the Only Dr.
        for Me," 64
    "Baltimore Oriole," 26
    "Barefoot in Baltimore," 70
    "Black, Brown and Beige," 100
    "Bread and Butter," 79
    "Crabs for Christmas," 12
    "Dog Bottom," 75
    "Elusive Butterfly," 27
    "How You Gonna' Keep 'em Down on
        the Farm?" 1
    "Huzza for the Constellation," 75
    "I'm Just Wild About Harry," 58
    "Jungle Man," 75
    "Little Criminals," 6
    "Lady Came from Baltimore, The," 67
    "Maryland, My Maryland," 35, 52, 87
    "My Blue Heaven," 1
    "My Buddy," 1
    "My Kind of Town, Chicago Is," 82
    "Minnie the Moocher," 91
    "Solitude," 100
    "Star-Spangled Banner," 15, 33, 37,
        42, 56, 79
    "Tannenbaum, O Tannenbaum," 67
    "When You Wish Upon a Star," 33
    "You've Got Sunshine on a Cloudy
        Day," 35
Southern High School, 71
Spade, Sam, 44, 60
Spectacular Bid, 3, 81
Sportin' Life, 84
Sporting Magazine, The, 87

Sports Illustrated, 83
Stamenkovic, Stan, 83
Starr, Blaze, 2, 24, 77
Stein, Gertrude, 3, 58, 70, 91
Stewart, Benjamin, 28
Stewart, Lucille Polk, 88
Stewart, William, 28
Stoker, Bram, 17
Stone, Steve, 92
Stratton, Charles Sherwood, 9
Strawberry Alarm Clock, 70
Streetcars, 30, 48
Submarine, 34, 35
Subway, 76
Sullivan, John L., 50
Sullivan, Margaret, 79
Sun Newsboy Band, 60
Sun Square, 26
Sunpapers, 10, 24, 25, 29, 30, 48, 53,
    58, 60, 78, 83, 87, 88, 92, 96, 98
Swampy Harbor Field, 55
Swarthmore, 26
Szold, Henrietta, 19
Szymanski, Dick, 99

T
Taney, Roger B., 77
Taussig, Helen Brooke, 50
Taylor, Robert, 96
Taylor, Zachary, 63
Telegraph, 56, 58, 100
Television:
    "All My Children," 78
    "Bosom Buddies," 45
    "Captain Kangaroo," 63
    CBS, 10, 25
    "Edge of Night," 32
    "Good Morning America," 10
    "Good Times," 6
    "Hot l Baltimore," 46, 61
    "I've Got a Secret," 54
    "Masquerade Party," 25
    "Mission Impossible," 86
    "On Our Own," 7
    "Person to Person," 56
    "Taxi," 61
    "The A Team," 75
    "The Jeffersons," 74
    "The Trial of the Catonsville Nine,"
        38
    "Three on a Match," 54
    "Tic Tac Dough," 87
    "To Tell The Truth," 54
    WBAL-TV, 17, 54
    WJZ-TV, 78
    WMAR-TV, 27, 94
Temporary insanity, 42
Tennis, 17
Thayer, Norman, Jr., 80
Three Rivers, 60
Three Stooges, 61

Thurston, Fred, 73
Times Theater, 43
Timmanus, E. Clay, 26
Titanic, 88
Tom Thumb, 9, 50
Torsk, 35
Touchdowners, 74
Towson State University, 70, 75
Tracy, Spencer, 32
Trahan, Burden and Charles, 79
Truman, Harry, 15, 34, 54, 72
Turk, Bob, 35
Two O'Clock Club, 2, 46, 57
Tydings, Millard, 34, 78

U
UCLA, 43
Ukulele, Ike, 33
Umbrellas, 5
Uncles, Charles Randolph, 44
Unglebower, Hoggie, 28
Union Party, 84
Union Reform Party, 58
Union Station, 76
Unitas, John, 2, 19, 30, 37, 47, 55, 63,
    89, 94, 99
United States Postal Service, 34, 63
University of Maryland, 7, 20, 31
Unseld, Wes, 78
Uris, Leon, 40, 69
U.S.S. Baltimore, 23, 52

V
Vagabond Players, 19
Vail, Alfred, 56
Valentino, Rudolph, 17
Van Buren, Martin, 24, 45, 60, 74

Vega, Luis "The Bull," 100
Verne, Jules, 54
Vietnam, 7
Vitamins, 48
Volstead Act of 1919, 61
von Rapf, Henrietta, 55
Voorhis, Jerry, 1

W
Wagner, Klaus, 96
Walbrook, 66
Walcott, Samuel T., 76
Walker, Jimmy, 6
Walker, Johnny, 62
Walt Disney Productions, 45
Walter Reed Army Medical Center, 42
War Admiral, 26, 89
Warden, Jack, 31
Warner Brothers, 28
Warren, Lavinia, 9
Washington College Hospital, 30
Washington, George, 2, 33, 40, 81, 82,
    98
Washington, Martha, 72
Washington Monument, 2, 28, 51, 83,
    98
Washington Press Club, 44
Waters, John, 72, 96
Watson, Dr. John B., 13
Watts, J. H. C., 98
Wauben, Mark, 92
Waverly, 14
Wayne, Ruth, 57
Weaver, Earl, 39, 50, 71, 92
WEBB, 3
Webb, Chick, 31, 75
Webster, Daniel, 24
Weinberg and Green, 73

Wells, David, 14
Wells, H.G., 56
West Point, 51, 55, 57, 62, 73
Westminster Graveyard, 67
WFBR Radio, 62
Whetstone, 42, 81
Whigs, 24, 37, 40, 63, 68
Whimsical, 47, 95
Whipping post, 21
Whirlaway, 10, 89
Widley, Thomas, 93
Willehad, 30
Williams, Edward Bennett, 39, 69
Wilson, Ellen Axson, 67
Wilson, Lanford, 61
Wilson, Woodrow, 13, 59, 67, 78
Windsor, Duchess of, 15, 56, 85
Windsor, Duke of, 56, 85
Winfrey, Oprah, 78
Winston, S. K., 68
Wolfe, Thomas, 9
Wood, Ron, 10
Woodford, Helen, 18
Woodhouse, Guy, 11
Woodhouse, Rosemary, 11
Woodhull, Victoria, 77
Woodlawn Vase, 75, 89, 95
World Cup, 10
Wyman Park, 36

Y
YMCA, 90
You Can't Go Home Again, 9

Z
Zappa, Frank, 22, 63
Zinman, David, 68
Zoo, 91

The author encourages anyone who has any special Baltimore trivia that they would like to share to forward their questions and answers, along with at least one verifiable source, to:

Dennis McClellan
c/o Schneidereith & Sons, Inc.
2905 Whittington Avenue
Baltimore, Maryland 21230